OPPOSITES

~~ATTRACT~~

ATTACK

**Turning Differences Into
Opportunities**

OPPOSITES

**Turning Your Differences
Into Opportunities**
••••••••••••••••••••••••
Jack & Carole Mayhall

NAVPRESS ◢●
A MINISTRY OF THE NAVIGATORS
P.O. BOX 6000, COLORADO SPRINGS, COLORADO 80934

The Navigators is an international Christian
organization. Jesus Christ gave His followers
the Great Commission to go and make disciples
(Matthew 28:19). The aim of The Navigators is
to help fulfill that commission by multiplying
laborers for Christ in every nation.

NavPress is the publishing ministry of The Navigators. NavPress publications are tools to help
Christians grow. Although publications alone cannot make disciples or change lives, they can help
believers learn biblical discipleship, and apply
what they learn to their lives and ministries.

Printed in the United States of America

Contents

To Lynn and Tim,
our daughter and son-in-law.

Two who have become one special couple and demonstrate:
. . . love in their lives,
. . . purpose in their service,
. . . eternity in their hearts.

We thank God upon every remembrance of you.

Authors

Jack Mayhall and his wife, Carole, have been with The Navigators since 1956. Jack has had a variety of responsibilities over the years, including seven years as the United States Director. Currently, Jack and Carole are ministering in the department of Marriage and the Family. They travel extensively in the United States and overseas, speaking to individuals and groups concerning marriage and discipleship.

Carole has a ministry with women nationwide. She is the author of several books, including *Lord of My Rocking Boat*; *Words that Hurt, Words that Heal*; and *Help Lord, My Whole Life Hurts*. She and Jack co-authored *Marriage Takes More Than Love*.

Acknowledgments

We especially want to thank:

Dr. Gary Jackson Oliver whose help in critiquing and evaluating this manuscript as it relates to the Myers-Briggs Type Indicator was invaluable.

Kathy Yanni, Traci Mullins, and Jean Stephens who are friends as well as editors.

All those special couples who have shared with us *their* differences.

We are grateful.

Preface

JACK

Please: Keep two factors in mind while you read this book.

One: Although we are writing primarily for husbands and wives, the broader applications for understanding differences go far beyond the bonds of marriage. They apply to almost any interpersonal relationship. I wish I had understood and realized the significance of some of these diversities years ago in relating to co-workers and teams of men and women as well as to friends and associates. So we hope you will think in broad sweeps while you look at the two brushstrokes we've selected.

Two: We are not presenting male/female differences, but *people* differences. Although some characteristics tend to be gender-related, we don't wish to categorize people. So, as you study yourself and your partner, if you find yourself departing from the "norm" (if there is such a thing!), *celebrate* your uniqueness. Let it be a freeing discovery for you.

There are as many personalities as there are people in the world today. Each person is *unique.* But we feel it is helpful to generalize personalities into types, preferences, and approaches in order to better understand ourselves, the people around us, and any possible exceptions we may run into.

May God open your mind and heart as you study and learn for a lifetime.

Introduction
SO WHAT'S THE DIFFERENCE?

CAROLE
The voice on the other end of the telephone identified herself as the daughter of a longstanding friend. After we chatted for a few minutes, she told me she and her husband had taken a type-indicator test the night before in preparation for a career change. I could have predicted her next remark. "We are so different in *everything*," she lamented.

"Great!" I replied.

There was a slight gasp on the other end of the phone followed by a long pause. "Do you think being so very different is *good*?"

"I really do," I responded. "Actually, we've only met a handful of couples who feel they have similar characteristics and responses. And we feel sorry for them."

"Why?" she queried.

"Because they are missing out," I continued. "If they are alike, they may have the same potential strengths, but they'll probably have similar weaknesses, too, which need to be identified and balanced by opposite types of personalities. Each personality has pluses with which to help others and minuses to be avoided—*with* the help of others.

"Several months ago, we talked with a couple—married only two years—who were mostly alike. Both were introverts, logical thinkers, plodders, goal-oriented, and organized. While there are some positive results in being similar, there are also some potentially negative ones.

Two negative results of being the same in these ways were a lack of social outreach and little ability to have fun together. Neither one had creative ideas for how to spend quality time together on dates and trips, nor did they have the motivation or incentive to go out. We're grateful that they recognized their need of stimulation from friends who are unlike them and have since taken steps to fill in those weak areas.

"But fortunately, most of us have God-given differences which, if we allow God to use them, help to complete us.

"Then, too, the truth of Proverbs 27:17 is less applicable if we are alike—'As iron sharpens iron, so one man sharpens another.' It's the *differences* that give the iron its roughness, its sharpening power. Marriage is one of God's best ways to hone us to become more like His Son."

She was silent for a moment. "Um . . . I see what you mean," she said. But I could tell she wasn't convinced that the differences were a positive and not a negative aspect of her marriage. That is understandable. Family counselor Dr. Gary Oliver says it well: "There are few who fight the law of gravity, but many who fight the law of differences."

Would you believe Jack and I have been married for forty years and are still discovering ways in which we are different—or variations of the same characteristic we'd never seen before? It's true. As we interact with more and more couples, we become increasingly convinced that the contrasts between husbands and wives are not only misunderstood, they are not accepted or even recognized. One writer put it this way:

> God's creation is remarkably diverse: from penguins to horses to Persian cats. Each feeds, mates, seeks shelter, but their sharp differences make for a fascinating world.
>
> People, too, are diverse. The principles for marriage may be the same for each couple: commitment, communication, shared values. But as we emphasize the commonalities, let's equally celebrate every couple as unique. If each person, made in God's image, is "a new thing under the sun"—a phenomenon—then two bonded together is also a marvel.[1]

A great many people refuse to believe their partners *are different.* And when they don't see their mates as different, the only alternative is to believe they are *wrong.*

How sad.

Why should we be surprised to find that we are diverse? Scripture plainly affirms that God *created* us to be different. A wonderful passage in 1 Corinthians 12 explains that each member of Christ's Body is unique. Let's read it with marriage partners in mind:

> Now the body is not made up of one part but of many. If the foot should say, "Because I am not a hand, I do not belong to the body," it would not for that reason cease to be part of the body. And if the ear should say, "Because I am not an eye, I do not belong to the body," it would not for that reason cease to be part of the body. If the whole body were an eye, where would the sense of hearing be? If the whole body were an ear, where would the sense of smell be? But in fact God has arranged the parts in the body, every one of them, just as he wanted them to be. If they were all one part, where would the body be? As it is, there are many parts, but one body.
>
> The eye cannot say to the hand, "I don't need you!" And the head cannot say to the feet, "I don't need you!" On the contrary, those parts of the body that seem to be weaker are indispensable, and the parts that we think are less honorable we treat with special honor. . . . But God has combined the members of the body . . . *so that there should be no division* in the body, but that its parts should have equal concern for each other. (Verses 14-25, emphasis mine)

God's plan is for great diversity, but with *no division* in the body of Christ. The same is true in the marriage relationship. Think of yourself and your spouse as two puzzle pieces fitting together. God created us to *complement* or complete each other. That's one purpose of marriage.

A second purpose is to place us in a situation in which change is demanded.

Our differences—when understood, appreciated, and allowed to be used by God—are those things God created for the great purpose of conforming us to the image of His Son (or, as Proverbs puts it, to "sharpen" one another). What do you get when iron rubs against iron? *Heat*. Sparks fly. But if the pieces are rubbed in the right way, they inevitably *sharpen* each other.

This process of rubbing lives together day after day, month after month, year after year, becomes God's change-agent—His refining tool to make us better people, to rub off the rough edges of our personalities, to give us understanding hearts, to teach us acceptance, to help us *change*. This change will occur *if* we choose to learn from each other. But if we remain rigid, we will thwart one of the great purposes of marriage.

Robert Runcie, Archbishop of Canterbury, gave a marvelous homily at the wedding of Prince Charles and Lady Diana. In it he said,

> Here is the stuff of which fairy tales are made, the prince and princess on their wedding day. But fairy tales usually end at this point with the simple phrase, "They lived happily every after." This may be because fairy tales regard marriage as an anticlimax after the romance of courtship. This is not the Christian view. Our faith sees the wedding day not as a place of arrival but the place where the adventure begins.[2]

David Seamands makes this penetrating statement: "Very few people look at their marriages as a commitment to growth—growing as an individual and of enabling one's partner to grow. Unless a husband and wife commit themselves to this kind of mutual growing *together*, they will grow *apart* and will not achieve the satisfying relationship of intimacy and love which they both deeply desire."[3]

The question then becomes, "Do I really *want* to grow—to change?"

If you answer yes to that question, then one of the first steps you should take is to find out who you are and to know—really *know*—the person you're married to.

Have you ever asked yourself the question, "What would I have to know in order to truly understand who I am? To understand the person I married?"

To begin answering this question, here are some areas you would need to explore:

Family background/environment/history/place in family/role models: These factors affect attitudes toward illness, death, gifts, vacations, holidays, work, recreation, culture and arts, racial issues, sexuality, sharing, showing affection, acceptance, serving, responsibilities.

Spiritual gifts/talents: What creative talents do you or your partner have? Have you been given the gift of mercy, teaching, serving, leadership, hospitality (etc.)? How do these gifts and talents work out in day to day living?

Personal identity in Christ: Head and heart knowledge of this crucial area affects many others, such as self-worth, Christ-worth (whether you feel worthless or loved), and struggles to perform versus resting in Christ.

Personality type: This area includes preferences, such as whether you are an introvert or extrovert; whether you take in information primarily through your five senses or sort it intuitively; whether you approach decisions with your head, as a thinker, or with your heart, as a feeler; whether your lifestyle tends to be organized and deliberate or flexible and spontaneous.

These areas comprise a very brief summary of the concept of personality type as presented in a widely-used test called the "Myers-Briggs Type Indicator," or the MBTI. If you aren't familiar with this indicator, please see the appendix for a fuller explanation of the MBTI. Take some time to read this section now, and you'll get a better understanding of some things we will be referring to in the next several chapters—although our discussion of differences in marriage partners does not adhere strictly to the MBTI definitions and preferences. Personality type is not the only path to understanding differences, but it is one of the best ways to see and identify them and so provides a helpful springboard.

These areas of exploration are no doubt only the *beginning* of learning who you are and who your spouse is. But they are a start. John Fischer comments, "The success of a marriage comes not in finding the 'right' person, but in the ability of both partners to adjust to the real person they inevitably realize they married. Some people never make this adjustment, becoming trapped in the endless search after an image that doesn't exist."[4] In order to adjust to the *real* person you married, you must know and understand yourself, and you must know and understand your partner.

A lawyer we know who handles many divorce cases and makes every effort he can to help couples reconcile their differences told Jack about the biggest problem he runs into: "People refuse to accept the fact that they are married to a *human being.* They have in mind at the outset that they are going to change this person they are marrying so they will become someone they can live with. After several years—or less—when their marriage partner doesn't change, they opt for divorce."

Paul Tournier identifies this central need in close relationships:

It is quite clear that between love and understanding there is a very close link. It is so close that we never know where the one ends and the other begins, nor which of the two is the cause or the effect. He who loves understands, and he who understands loves. One who feels understood feels loved, and one who feels loved feels sure of being understood.

No one can develop freely in this world and find a full life without feeling understood by at least one person. . . . To fail to understand one's spouse is to fail to understand oneself. It is also a failure to grow and to fulfill one's possibilities.[5]

Understanding and appreciating differences is what this book is all about. Our desire is for you to begin to understand yourself and your marriage partner. But we don't want you to stop there. We want you to know and understand the contrasts between you, accept what can't be changed, and change in ways that will help you be more like Jesus. We want you to see how these very differences can complete you as a couple, work for you, make you see and live and experience life in a richer way. And we want to give you practical means not only to discover who you are, but to find useful ways to fit together, to appreciate each other, to praise God for what and who you are as a couple.

May this book be more than an interesting read (though of course we want it to be that)—may it be a means by which you begin to make a study for the rest of your life. A study to *know* one another. A commitment to *understand* . . .

 and *adjust* . . .

 and *change.*

NOTES:
1. Harold L. Myra, "Conan or Cosby," *Marriage Partnership* (Spring 1988), page 48.

2. David A. Seamands, "The Royal Romance and Yours," quoted in *Asbury Seminary Herald* (September-October 1981).
3. Seamands, "The Royal Romance and Yours."
4. John Fischer, "The Image," *Partnership* (January-February 1988).
5. Paul Tournier, *To Understand Each Other* (Atlanta: John Knox Press, 1967), pages 28-29.

1
Who Shook
the Foundations?
FINDING THE RIGHT PLACE TO START

Nancy glanced down at the floor as she spoke slowly to the waiting group, comfortably seated in the living room.

"I guess my question is, have I learned anything? Are *we*, as a so-called Christian nation, learning anything? It seems like . . ." she hesitated and then continued, "well, like a Black Plague of broken marriages—and it's epidemic across most countries of the world. The death toll mounts every day but nobody seems to know what to *do* about it. Dave and I were divorced last year and I'm actually afraid—afraid to get married again; afraid to be hurt like that again if it doesn't work out; afraid of the fickleness of love, I guess. There certainly aren't any guarantees these days!"

Across the room, Bob nodded in agreement. "You're right, Nancy. No one seems immune to the disease. There is more stuff available today to help marriages succeed than ever before in history—books, counselors, studies of one kind or another, conferences and seminars, audio and video tapes—yet fewer couples are making it for the long haul. A friend of mine recently told me of a survey at a major midwestern university indicating that over fifty percent of the student body come from divorced homes."

He patted his wife's knee as he ventured, "Sue heard this week of the mother of one of her dearest friends who left her husband after forty-five years of marriage for a much younger man. Her husband—and his work in a Christian institution—have been deeply hurt, her children and grandchildren are devastated, but even more, she's shattered everything she's taught and lived for all her life. It's . . . well, it's sick!"

Anne glanced around the room and then burst out, "But why? Isn't there any hope for us? I have to admit, I'm scared too. Oh, Jim and I are happy right now, but what if it doesn't last? The future seems awfully shaky. Are *all* foundations crumbling? Or maybe there weren't any foundations in the first place. Maybe marriages in the past were only held together by the attitudes of society about divorce. Now that those have changed, we're falling apart. I feel like I not only don't have any answers, but I'm afraid I don't even know the right *questions*."

Jim sighed. "Well, I think the foundations that marriage should be based on are still in place—and still solid. It isn't the foundations that have shifted. *We* have. We place unsure bets on relationships built on sand in the first place."

Nancy flinched. "You'll have to explain *that*, Jim."

Jim grew reflective. "I guess what I mean is . . . well, take my Mom and Dad, Frank and Martha, who are here visiting with us." He motioned to a white-haired couple sitting together on the couch just in back of the circle of chairs. "They've been married for forty-five years, and it hasn't always been easy. They've had their struggles just like everybody else. But to them divorce was never an option. So the commitment to work through difficulties *forced* them to do just that. And in struggling through them, they grew."

"Today, we *say* we're committed, but I think in the back of our minds there is always that option to go to Plan B—if it doesn't seem to be working, we can get a divorce. So in the midst of major fights, the effort needed to push through doesn't seem worthwhile."

Dan frowned. "That's true, Jim, but some of us thought we were committed and still didn't make it."

Sally broke in. "Kevin and I have been married for thirteen years now, and one thing we've discovered is that a relationship takes more work than we ever dreamed possible! Nothing prepared us for that, but it makes sense when you realize how much time you have to spend working on other things that are important to you."

"I know what you mean!" Dan exclaimed. "If most people gave five percent of the time, effort, and thought to their marriages that they do to their careers, they'd really have much happier and deeper relationships."

The group was silent for a few moments, and then Nancy turned to Jim's parents. "Frank and Martha, you've been sitting there not saying a word, but I have a feeling you could give us some good advice." She grinned and added, "After all, you've been married for longer than most of us have lived! Jim tells us that you have a happy marriage—and I, for one, would like to hear how you've done it."

Each member of the group chimed in their invitation. Within a few minutes, fresh coffee steaming in cups around the room, they settled into an expectant hush.

Frank cleared his throat. "If I remember correctly, you started out talking about foundations . . . ."

Nancy nodded at Frank's inquiring look.

"If you are going to talk about foundations," he went on, "I'm thinking you have to begin with the Bible. And if you are going to talk about foundations in marriage, you also have to begin with the Bible. There's a verse in Isaiah 33:6 that talks about *the foundation*. It says, 'He [God] will be the *sure* foundation for your times, a rich store of salvation and wisdom and knowledge; the fear of the LORD is the key to this treasure.'"

Sally broke in. "Well, *that* certainly is succinct, isn't it?"

Frank nodded. "Yes, it is. And these words are as valid today as they were when they were written roughly 2700 years ago. The eternal truth is that God will be—that is, if we let Him, for He won't force His way into our lives or marriages—*the sure foundation*. The *only* sure foundation."

Frank looked at each person in the room as he continued, "A foundation is the base upon which something rests. God is the base—our life is the 'something' resting on it. If we let God be the base on which our life rests, He will become a rich store of salvation—meaning deliverance, aid, victory, prosperity, help, wisdom, and knowledge. Who of us who is married doesn't need that kind of input . . . daily?"

The group nodded in agreement.

"It seems to me," Frank went on, "that it borders on impertinence or even arrogance to leave God out of the equation in our marriages.

"After all, He invented it! Marriage was God's idea and therefore He needs to be given His rightful place in that relationship.

"So we're back to foundations again. Genesis means 'beginning' or 'origin,' and we need to go to the book of Genesis to find the origin of marriage."

Frank reached for his worn Bible, opened it to the first book, and read aloud from the second chapter, verses 18-25. After finishing the account, he looked up and commented, "From the beginning, God intended marriage to be a triangle of entities—the husband, the wife, and God. If we leave God out of His rightful place, we have left out the rich store of salvation and wisdom and knowledge Isaiah refers to as a *treasure*. And it states that the fear of the Lord—a profound awareness of God—is the key to this treasure."

Frank put his Bible down on the table beside him and glanced at Martha. Squeezing her hand, he said, "I remember when we were married in a small white-frame church many years ago. I can still hear the minister cautioning us even before the ceremony, 'You two are very much in love, and I'm glad for that! But remember there is a room in the heart that is so remote it can only be reached by God alone. If it is not filled by God there will always be a wistful feeling of longing. Being in love may drown this for a while, but inevitably it returns and its presence mars the sweetness and blights the romance. So love each other with all your hearts, but love God more. Never forget that it is not the love of man or woman that satisfies a human heart. It is only the love of God that fills all the empty spaces.'"

A smile wreathed Frank's face as he went on, "But the mystery is, while God is the supplier of love and worth, He has so made us to need and complete each other as well. Martha and I learned much about *that* the hard way. We started out so—well, so very *different*."

He stopped speaking. Martha caught the silent message that he wanted her to continue and took a deep breath. She, too, was thinking back—of early struggles, first commitments, a lifetime of learning that it takes to make a marriage. "We've had our share of difficulties, haven't we, Frank?"

Martha looked around at the group of earnest faces. "Oh, the stories I could tell you! It was painful learning at times, I'll tell you *that*. But one really important lesson we learned grew out of an article I read about 'How to Get Alone With Your Husband.' It became almost a game to find ways of getting unexpected time alone together. I even recruited the children's help to synchronize their nights out! We invented a 'Don't

Go to Meeting' night and also made Saturday morning a breakfast out time for just the two of us because that was the day we had to go to town for supplies anyway. We discovered that many days we'd been *around* each other, but not *with* each other. We finally committed ourselves to the fact that quality communion with our closest friend is a need we were both created with—because that uncompromised time with a life partner is a quiet center too precious to neglect."[1]

She paused and Sally broke in. "That's *it*! That's what I was saying before. When we got married, we had no idea how much *work* it would take to maintain and develop a good relationship. Isn't that what you're saying? That working at your marriage in a hundred ways is part of the elusive 'commitment' word?"

Martha and Frank both nodded as he exclaimed, "Exactly! And *time for each other* is a great part of that commitment. Personally, Martha and I had to exert a lot of effort for this, what with the farm and the kids and church all vying for our time and attention. We talked about the need to set aside priority time with each other. For us, it meant fifteen minutes after the chores were done and supper was cooking—on the porch in summer or in the parlor in winter—and the kids knew what the closed door of the parlor meant! We committed ourselves to take some time out of the house each week to be alone together in a special way. It didn't happen overnight, but we learned how to work at our marriage! We learned to laugh at ourselves and with each other. We learned the importance of little things, too—those thoughtful small courtesies so important to staying in love."

The two of them smiled thoughtfully at each other. Then Frank commented, "But you know—we talk a good deal about commitment these days—to love, to understand, to accept, to learn, to laugh together, to work through conflict, to grow—all these are essential. But one thing that's not talked about a lot is faithfulness. It has to *mean* something when two people pledge before God and witnesses that they will love and cherish *only* each other."

"And dear friends," Martha interjected, her eyes glistening with tears, "please understand that we never would have made it without commitment. Commitment to each other, yes; but a commitment to God is even more important. We never would have made it without His help!"

Frank put his arm around Martha and concluded, "I guess that's what's been eroded in these past years around the world. Some never lay that 'sure foundation' in the first place. Others have the foundation in place but fail to sink the stakes of commitment and faithfulness into that foundation—and, of course, the structure will fall in the frequent storms unless both the foundation and the supports are strong.

"It's God—the foundation—who teaches us control when we're angry; He teaches us unselfishness when every fiber in us wants what *we* want. He not only gives us a reason for living and a hope in dying, He gives us a fullness of life that transcends the everydayness of living. Faith, hope, and love are meaningless words without God."

Before they broke for dessert and coffee, Nancy verbalized the thoughts of the group. "Thank you," she said simply. "You've given us—you've given me, at least—something I've needed for a long time. You've given me. . . ." There was a pause and then she added one word filled with expression, "*Hope.*"

✦ ✦ ✦

In this book, we're going to concentrate on one specific aspect of growth in marriage—understanding and balancing and completing each other to make our differences join together to help rather than frustrate. But as we focus on this one facet, may we be ever conscious that without God the building will collapse. Without commitment, the structure will be destroyed. Without faithfulness, love will perish. God holds the key. In reality, He *is* the key.

Keeping that in mind . . .

Let's begin.

NOTE:
1. Taken from material in Ron Hutchcraft, "Huddle Time," *Partnership* (July-August 1985), page 39.

PART I

THE WAY WE THINK

2

What You Think, How I Feel

FACTUAL VS. INTUITIVE

From the very beginning of our marriage, we have laughed about some things.

And fought over others.

After many years we laugh about more. But continue to cry over a few.

Still we say, "Thank God for differences!"

They exasperate, but intrigue; frustrate, yet attract. We moan and groan, thunder and wonder at the extent and variety of them.

It has been said that God gave us two eyes in order to see things from more than one point of view. With only one eye, we lose dimension. We see the world as flat. But with two eyes, we gain dimension and see the world as round.

We say, *Vive la différence.*

Let's begin with a major one!

JACK

The opening paragraphs of the book got my attention:

If I do not want what you want, please try not to tell me that my want is wrong.

Or if I believe other than you, at least pause before you correct my view.

Or if my emotion is less than yours, or more, given the same circumstances, try not to ask me to feel more strongly or weakly.

. . . I do not, for the moment at least, ask you to understand me. That will come only when you are willing to give up changing me into a copy of you.

. . . If you will allow me any of my own wants, or emotions, or beliefs, or actions, then you open yourself, so that some day these ways of mine might not seem so wrong, and might finally appear to you as right—for me. To put up with me is the first step to understanding me. Not that you embrace my ways as right for you, but that you are no longer irritated or disappointed with me for my seeming waywardness. And in understanding me you might come to prize my differences from you, and, far from seeking to change me, preserve and even nurture those differences.[1]

Right now, somewhere in the world, there are two people heating up in discussion who need to stop and consider those paragraphs. Their words sound something like this: One person (most likely a man) is saying in an accusatory tone, "But that's not what you *said*!" And the other person (most likely a woman) is saying, "Honey, I can't tell you why, but *I just feel there's something wrong*."

We grit our teeth. We sigh. We roll our eyes. We bite our tongue and try to control our response to our difference. And we get frustrated mainly because we fail to understand—*really* understand.

One of our struggles is with facing the *fact* (that tells you where I'm coming from!) that there are two basic ways to take in information, to perceive what is going on around us. Some of us take in information by way of the five senses—sight, sound, touch, taste, and smell. Others of us process information by way of a sixth sense—a hunch or, as we usually call it, *intuition*.

Years ago, Carole and I realized we differ in our approach to what we see around us. For instance, to me a fact is a fact is a fact. I want to start at the beginning and take things one step at a time. I identify with a statement such as, "Most problems precisely defined are already partially solved."[2]

To Carole, a fact is slightly more or less than a fact, depending on what mood she's in. She agrees with a statement such as, "A single fact will often spoil an interesting argument."[3] She tends to jump in anywhere and leap over steps. I must admit, this approach is confusing to me.

I read instructions and notice details to process those instructions while Carole often skips directions and just—tries it. In fact, it's become a family joke. When something goes wrong with one of our household appliances and Carole is standing there in exasperation, she glances in my direction, grins sheepishly and says, "I know. I know. When all else fails, *read the instructions*."

I like set procedures, established routines, things that are definite and measurable. A practical thinker, I often ask, "Will it work? And if not, why not?" Carole enjoys change and variety, prefers to imagine possibilities, and likes opportunities to be inventive and creative. She'll try something to *see* if it works—and if it doesn't, she won't worry about it.

This difference is a tough one to come to grips with and, according to one clinical psychologist, places the widest gulf between people.[4]

One of the reasons for the difficulty in this area is that different ways of gathering data (factual vs. intuitive) can lead to an awareness of dissimilar data, or a contrasting pool of information. In some ways, this one personality characteristic is the most fundamental function, because it involves how we take in the information that becomes our raw material for how we look out at life, and what we look for when we look out.[5] To a great extent the way we take in information provides the data we use to make decisions and this can produce vast differences between a husband and a wife.

The Myers-Briggs study assured us that almost everyone jumps back and forth between these two approaches, but one is usually *preferred* and *better developed*.

Paul Tournier puts it this way, "An intuitive mind and a scientific mind [i.e.; factual] will have great difficulty in understanding each other. For the former, things are not what they objectively are, but rather symbols of other values which he imagines and associates with them. For the latter, things are precisely what they are, nothing but that which can be measured and weighed."[6]

One person wants facts, trusts facts, remembers facts. He believes in experience and processes information through what has happened to him and to others. This person notices and wants to deal with the actual—not the what-if's or the what-might-have-been's. He is a practical (should I say hard-headed?) realist. (I'm using the masculine here because that's the way I am—but some women have this tendency as well.)

The intuitive person doesn't gather information that way! Facts aren't as important as *impressions*. That's probably why inwardly I raise my eyebrows at some of Carole's "facts." She'll admit she sometimes makes up statistics—though she's quick to say if she has—and exaggerates at other times. Intuitive people like Carole are often theoretical and imaginative.

I've seen a number of factual-minded men get impatient with their intuitive wives. They are the kind of men who shake their heads in frustration, sometimes belittle their wives, and say to themselves (and occasionally out loud), "Intuition? What a dumb way to operate!" But another man stated, "Good instincts usually tell you what to do long before your head has figured it out."[7] At least one man appreciates the fine art of intuition!

If only we could be convinced that one way of thinking is not *wrong*. It's just *different*. And actually, we need both in order to complete each other.

We've observed that an intuitive person rarely gets disgusted with the factual person. Factual people get frustrated, however, when they can't get facts or details from the intuitive one.

Let's Identify

KEY WORDS[8]

Factual	Intuitive
deduction	intuition
details	patterns
present	future
practical	imaginative
facts	innovations
sequential	random
directions	hunches
repetition	variety
enjoyment	anticipation
perspiration	inspiration

(KEY WORDS, continued)

Factual	Intuitive
conserve	change
verify	invent
collect facts	synthesize theories
observe details	detect possibilities
likes the compass	uses the stars

How do you look at a house you are thinking of buying? Your answer may be a good indicator of whether you are a factual person or an intuitive one. I look at the square footage, how the rooms are arranged, and the conditions of the furnace, hot water heater, walls, and roof. Then I look at the conditions of the loan, the financing, how much upkeep there will be and how much work on the lawn.

Not Carole! To her, the house has to go "Booong" or she won't even look at it twice. When I ask her what kind of house will go "Booong," do you think she can tell me? No way. It just *has* to go "Booong."

But then, Carole can see the possibilities where I can't. She envisions what it will look like when she's through getting the rooms painted and the furniture in. I see—well, I see *the house* for what is there.

Both approaches have advantages. I face the facts; Carole discovers the possibilities. I'm realistic; Carole sees the unexplored options. I find out exactly what the situation is; Carole thinks about what might happen that has not happened before.

You see, Carole and I can go into a situation and see two completely different sets of things. Carole intuitively picks up on that raised eyebrow, the tone of voice, the body posture—nonverbal things.

So after a time with a couple, for example, I will ask Carole, "How did you *feel* about that situation?" She is unable to tell me what she actually observed that led to her feeling, but she tells me how she feels about our time with them.

I filter her response through my very practical grid and add to it the set of facts I've observed. Together we come up with a much better picture than either one of us could have done by ourselves.

We've learned much this way. About ourselves. About others. About life. About God. *Particularly* about God.

Carole especially has had to learn that many times God teaches us to stand on the facts of His Word and not go by what we are feeling at the moment.

For our thirty-fifth wedding anniversary, it seemed as though God had brought to reality a dream we'd had for several years—a chance to take a trip to England with our daughter and her husband, Tim. Then, at the very last minute, Tim developed kidney stones and they could not join us. Here is a portion of the letter Carole wrote to them afterward:

> I'm not sure I can write this without becoming teary again, but I'll try not to get drops all over my writing.
>
> I'm sure, like you perhaps, my main problem is not that God said "no" on the terrific bonus we'd asked Him for, but that He said "yes" all along the way and then just as we were about to taste the delicious morsel, seemingly smashed it and ground it under His heel. That is the way it looks from our human vantage point. And I'm saying, "Hey—I wouldn't do that to *my* child. How come You are doing it to four of Yours?"
>
> It is another missing piece, isn't it? Over and over, my head has had to remind my heart, "God *is* loving. That is a *fact*, not a feeling. He does all things *well* and He does all things in *love*." My heart says, "Really?" My head answers, "Truly." And my *will* responds, "Then I *will* praise You, Father, even in this."
>
> But wow! Is it hard!
>
> The first night [of a conference we were involved in] a message was given on Psalm 23 and we were reminded of an illustration Elisabeth Elliot uses about shepherds having to dip their sheep into horrible-smelling sheep disinfectant to get rid of all the ticks and insects which could cause them harm. The sheep have to go completely under several times and they struggle and fight and surely can't understand the seeming cruelty of the shepherd.
>
> Well, that's the picture that comes to mind. I'm struggling and kicking and not understanding. But He still is the *good* shepherd!

Carole is working at getting her intuitive emotions together with the facts. And I'm working to bring inspiration as well as perspiration into my thinking.

We *need* each other's help on this one!
But then, you already know that!

NOTES:

1. David Keirsey and Marilyn Bates, *Please Understand Me* (Del Mar, CA: Prometheus Nemesis Books, 1978), page 1.

2. Harry Lorayne, quoted in "Quotable Quotes," *Readers Digest* (November 1988), page 33.

3. From *Selected Cryptograms III*, quoted in "Quotable Quotes," page 33.

4. Keirsey and Bates, page 17.

5. From seminar notes by Dr. Gary Oliver.

6. Paul Tournier, *To Understand Each Other* (Atlanta: John Knox Press, 1967), page 37.

7. Michael Burke, quoted in "Quotable Quotes," *Readers Digest* (March 1987), page 17.

8. Word lists adapted by Dr. Gary Oliver from *Looking At Type*, by Earle C. Page (Gainesville, FL: C.A.P.T., 1983).

3

Two Sides of a Coin
LOGICAL VS. RELATIONAL

JACK

I have to admit it: I'm just a logical guy. I'm a problem solver who reaches conclusions step by reasonable step. I can't help myself. That's the way I think.

One Christmas, a friend gave us a ball-bearing clock—an ingenious thing, which took until midnight to put together. (And it took a lot of logic to *get* it together.) The clock has three slanting troughs with sixty little balls for minutes and twelve larger balls for hours. It's wired together so that every minute, one little ball drops into a lower trough until, on the hour, all of the balls slide down to push one hour ball to its time slot. It's fun to watch all the balls move at precisely twelve o'clock.

This timepiece fascinates me—it's inventive and logical.

Sometimes, I can almost feel my brain operating like that clock. You drop a problem-ball into my cognitive clock-mind and the process begins.

Methodically. Precisely. Surely.

The problem slides from one trough to another until all the balls fall into place and the solution brings high noon!

If I had a cutaway of Carole's deciding processes, my guess is that it would show a maze of wires going in every direction—electricity jumping from one place to another with rapid changes of current direction.

Yet, interestingly enough, Carole could quite possibly come up with the same solution to the problem as I would—and much more quickly! Of course, she wouldn't be able to explain the *process*—but then, she wouldn't consider it important to do so.

The difficulty, from my point of view, is twofold. First, if she were wrong, she wouldn't be able to find out where she went wrong because there is no identifiable *process*. Second, if she's *right*, she can't explain her thinking—at least not to a logical thinker like me.

Tough one! And, in our observation, not uncommon. In fact, Paul Tournier asserts, "Instinctively, a very rational man is going to marry a very sentimental woman. Their complementing one another will, at the beginning, elicit an enthusiastic reaction in him. But later on he will want to make her listen to the objective arguments of reason; he will become annoyed at not being successful in this. He will try to show her that she is not logical in her sentimental explosions. This does not worry her at all. On her part, she will reproach her husband for his ice-cold rational manner which stifles all life."[1]

As Carole and I interact with many couples, we find some very logical women and some very sensitive men. If you fall into these patterns, praise God for it. However, most times the men we meet are logical, rational types and the women are the feeling, sensitive ones.

There may be physiological reasons for this generalized difference between women and men. Many people these days are attributing the logical/feeling differences to the fact that some people (usually males) operate predominantly out of the left side of their brain while others (usually female) either operate more from the right side or have a balance of both. According to family counselor H. Norman Wright, "The thinking pattern of the left side of your brain is positive, analytical, linear, explicit, sequential . . . concrete, rational and goal-oriented. The right side is intuitive, spontaneous, emotional . . . visual, artistic, playful, holistic and physical."[2] The left side wants to know "What's the bottom line?" and the right side travels around the barn a few times to get there.

Check out a couple at a football game, especially one in which their son is playing! The woman is mentally chewing on a handkerchief with worry over her boy getting injured while the man is yelling his head off for his son to score.

This poem, called "Mom and Dad At The Game," elicited a laugh from both Carole and me:

They claim the sexes
    are the same,
But check them
    at the football game.

He notes the gain of every yard;
She worries that they hit too hard.

They drop the ball
    and how he grumbles?
She pities everyone who fumbles.

He finds the halftime show
    a bore;
She'd like the band to play
    some more.

Girls twirl. He smiles,
    forgets to scold.
She wonders if their legs are cold.

Two minutes. There's a pass
    complete,
A touchdown made
    he's on his feet.

"That's it!" he cries. "There
    goes the gun.
Now watch our boys go wild.
    We won!"

Why must she think, at such
    an hour,

Of *their* boys crying in the
    shower?
—Helene Lewis Coffer[3]

When I was playing high school football, a teammate told me of
a remark his mother had made after one of our games. It was fourth
down, and she watched as I tried to kick the ball. Three times the
opposing team went offsides and blocked my kick; three times the
penalty was called and I tried again. I finally succeeded on the fourth
attempt.

After the game, my friend's mother asked him with genuine concern, "*Why* wouldn't they let Jack kick that ball?" I can still remember
all of us cracking up over her limited football knowledge and her moth-
erly concern. Now I know better! There really is more than one way of
looking at things!

Some experts say that while we all shift back and forth from
one side of the brain to the other, a man's brain is likely to be more
highly specialized. A woman operates more wholistically, with both
sides functioning at once. This means a man can give more focused
attention to what he is doing, but a woman, using both sides of her
brain simultaneously to work on a problem, has an advantage.

And no wonder! One study indicates that women have more "connectors" between the two sides even as infants and thus can integrate
information more skillfully. (Not fair, right guys?) This apparently
enables them to tune in to everything going on around them—like
cooking dinner, listening to one child practice scales on the piano,
helping another write a letter to Santa Claus, and talking on the phone
all at the same time—while her husband complains that he can't read
the paper because one child is banging two potlids together in the
next room.

One result of a woman having additional connectors is that she may
be extra perceptive about people. She picks up feelings and connects
them more readily to what she is thinking.

If these studies are correct—that women have extra connectors—then this means *a woman's expectation of a man's perceptual
ability should be tempered with such knowledge.*[4] In other words,
women need to have great patience and understanding of men's difficulty in handling multiple things or in expressing emotions readily.

But men need patience, too—to understand and accept the feelings of their wives.

When Carole and I took the Myers-Briggs Type Indicator, it confirmed what we already knew! We were greatly different in three areas; alike—sort of—in the fourth. The indicator stated that the difference between a logical approach and a feeling or relational approach (in MBTI language, the "Thinker vs. the Feeler") represented two ways of deciding on and evaluating information. The one person functions by deciding things on the basis of logic and objective considerations—which describes me. I probably decide things more with my head, and I want to know what the "real truth" is about something before I decide. I tend to be an onlooker, viewing things from outside the situation, and I take an overall view.

The feeling-oriented person decides on the basis of personal, subjective values. That describes Carole, who most often makes decisions with her heart. She goes by personal convictions and is concerned for relationships and harmony. She is almost always a participant within the situation and takes an immediate and personal view.

I need Carole's approach as a balance to my logical, impersonal, objective mode.

Just recently we were invited to two different open houses on a Sunday afternoon the day after we had arrived home from an extensive trip. My inclination was to hibernate at home and watch the golf tournament on TV. But we went to the open house for a departing missionary and the engagement party for a friend's daughter. Why? Because I chose to rely on Carole's sensitivity to people and her perception of the importance of relationships in spite of the way I was feeling.

CAROLE

I must admit, there have been years of my life when I not only didn't understand Jack's way of approaching life in certain instances, I didn't *appreciate* it.

But the more years we live together, the more I see why God led us together. I am realizing the ways I need Jack and perhaps why God made many men to be this logical kind of critter.

Not too long ago we were involved in a distressing situation that put my emotional circuits on overload. That same week, we were speaking every morning at a conference. Jack sensed that it was all I could do

to keep my emotions under control. On the second day of the conferences, he said to me, "Honey, we've *got* to stay somewhat detached in
this situation for the next two weeks so we can give ourselves to these
conferences."

Inwardly I thought, "*How* am I going to do that?" But before I
could voice my question, he added, "The next time our friend calls,
just say, 'Let me have you talk to Jack.' I want to protect you in this."

Gratefully, I responded, "I'll do that."

As I was going up the stairs, I thought, "How wonderful it is to
have a husband who has a greater capacity for this kind of situation
than I do because he can be less emotional about it than I. He *can* stay
detached. He can distance himself."

Formerly, I had resented that distancing ability, but now I thought,
"It's great to have someone to depend on who is steadier than I am;
to take responsibility; to 'hold me back.' But who does *Jack* have?
He has the Lord, of course. And he can share things with me. But
what flesh-and-blood person does he have to whom he can pass the
emotional load?" And I answered my own question, "No one!"

Jack, as the head of the family, as a mature adult, has no one to
pass the buck to. He has the ultimate responsibility.

That day it struck me as never before how necessary it is that he
isn't as emotional as I am. If he were, he might "bomb out" at critical
points in our life together. I know I would!

Two weeks before this incident, we had talked with a couple who
were our exact opposites. He had been a pilot in the U. S. Air Force a
couple of years before and at one point had been assigned as the escort
officer for a friend who had been killed in an air crash. His task was to
accompany the body back to the States and to be of help to the widow
and her family.

Dan was a sensitive man, very aware of the hurts and needs of
those around him. During the week he was with the grieving family, he
became immersed in their situation. Emotionally, he became husband
and father to the widow and her children as well as bereaved friend.

When Dan flew back to be with his family the day before Thanksgiving, he collapsed! He was so emotionally depleted he couldn't relate
to his own wife and family. His wife was not only hurt but jealous of
his deep involvement with another wife and family.

As we talked with them, we realized that God had given Dan a

precious gift. He could identify and empathize and be inv_._
way that most men could not. But along with the gift came certain
dangers that he needed to guard against with extreme care. There
were two in particular: he would have to protect his own emotional
resources so that giving to other people would not so drain him that
he had nothing left for his own wife and children. And he would have
to be extremely cautious that his emotional *involvement* with others did
not lead to emotional *entanglements*.

Afterward I thought about the times I'd heard wives say, "Oh, my
husband doesn't seem to *feel* deeply. He can't relate to my emotions. I
wish he were like . . . [a pastor, a counselor, a friend]." I considered
the times I'd had to stop my own thoughts from going in that direction.
And I went to Jack right then and there and apologized to him.

Then I had a special praise service to a God who created a husband
with exactly the characteristics I need. "Thank You, God," I prayed,
"for giving me a man who can take a detached view of circumstances,
of people—yes, of my emotions. One who can help me get perspective, who can take responsibility because he is able to stay cool and
levelheaded. Thank You, thank You, for Jack."

JACK

You can see that it's taken us some time to understand and appreciate
the other's approach to life. This is a critical difference: We hope it
won't take you as long as it's taken us.

It's necessary to see how we fit together as logical or feeling persons—to realize that the logical person's strength comes in analyzing
plans, seeing cause and effect, weighing the consequences and counting
the costs of all the options open. The feeling person, however, examines
how deeply people feel about the options, what values are involved,
what the needs are of those involved, and can make a fresh appraisal by
understanding how in the long run each solution will affect the people
involved.

Carole, as the primarily sensitive person, spontaneously *appreciates*; while I, being the logical one, have to be careful that I don't find
flaws and criticize.

Author Earle C. Page suggests that a logical person may seem cold
and condescending to the emotional one, while the emotional person
may seem fuzzy-minded to the logical one.[5]

I have to admit that in our early years, Carole and I focused more on the disadvantages of thinking differently than on appreciating each other's ways of viewing situations. But now we see how desperately we need each other.

Let's Identify

Who are you, and what kind of person are you married to? Take a moment to examine these key words[6] that describe each way of functioning.

Logical	Emotional
Thinking	Feeling
Head	Heart
Justice	Harmony
Cool	Caring
Impersonal	Personal
Analyze	Empathize
Precise	Persuasive
Principles	Values

In the next few chapters, we'll continue to consider the way we *think*. The lines between some of these functions are somewhat blurred—if you're a logical thinker, this may bother you. Please don't let it. Try to see the differences overall, and avoid making fine distinctions about the words themselves.

And, of course, you'll find that none of us is consistent. All of us (well, certainly most of us) use both logic and feelings in making decisions. But one approach usually characterizes the overall pattern.

As you look at these differences between you and your partner, say with us, "Thank You, Lord, for our diversity. Thank You that we aren't alike in this area. Thank You that You are working in our contrasts to shape us and conform us to Yourself. Thank You that You use these differences to make us to see Your world . . . *round*!"

Pray with us that God will open our eyes to the wonder—the incredible phenomenon—of being *one* even as we are different. Of having unity even in our diversity.

NOTES:
1. Paul Tournier, *To Understand Each Other* (Atlanta: John Knox Press, 1967), page 37.
2. H. Norman Wright, *Understanding the Man in Your Life* (Waco, TX: Word Books, 1987), page 28.
3. Helene Lewis Coffer, "Mom and Dad At The Game," *Good Housekeeping* (September 1981), page 99.
4. Earle C. Page, *Looking At Type* (Gainesville, FL: C.A.P.T., 1983).
5. Page, *Looking At Type*.
6. Page, *Looking At Type*.

4

It Just Depends on Where You're Standing
OBJECTIVE VS. SUBJECTIVE

CAROLE

All week long during the women's staff conference at Colorado's Glen Eyrie Conference Center, I had been "revving up." Seeing so many friends stimulated me more and more each day. I realized I was hyper, but I didn't give it much thought.

On Friday, we met the plane from Detroit and greeted a special nephew and his wife, who were flying in for the marriage seminar scheduled right after the women's conference. My motor accelerated. That evening before the seminar, we sat at a table for five couples, most of them strangers to one another, and my hostess-hospitality button got pushed along with my already stimulated talk-too-fast button. I could feel Little Miss Chatterbox picking up speed.

Then, under the table, I felt Jack's hand press my knee. I received his message instantly. "Carole," he was saying, "simmer down."

When Jack is nervous, he becomes increasingly quiet. When I get nervous—or excited, or stimulated in a variety of ways—I start talking faster and faster.

I realized that tendency. And so, when Jack sent his nonverbal signal . . . I tried.

On Saturday, between speaking and relating to friends and loved ones, my RPMs continued to rise. Several times Jack leaned close and said quietly, "Honey, simmer down."

47

Then at last we were alone in our room, ready to collapse from the day's activities.

But, of course, between my highly charged battery and my feelings about Jack's reminders, I knew there would be no sleep for me.

So I put my arms around Jack and the following conversation took place:

Carole: Do you love me?

Jack: Why, of course I love you.

Carole: I need that assurance right now.

Jack: For what reason?

Carole: Sometimes I guess I feel like you do love me, but maybe you don't *like* me at times.

Jack: What has given you that impression? What have I done that would cause you to feel that way?

Carole: Well, several times today you've told me to quiet down.

Jack: But you've been hyper all day—I was trying to help you.

Carole: I think I know that, but when it's *several times*, I think you can't like me when I'm that way.

Jack: But you need to accept the fact that the reason is that I want to *help* you.

Carole: (sighing) My head does. My heart doesn't always.

Jack: Honey, I love you, and I like you.

Would you believe I got up an hour later, tired as I was, to write down that conversation verbatim? I did it because it struck me that there were several significant things going on in it.

First, Jack kept probing and asking the right questions. If he hadn't done that, I wouldn't have told him what was really going on inside.

Second, I determined, humiliating to me as it was, to be honest and vulnerable about how I was feeling.

But third, it occurred to me that even in that exchange, we were approaching a situation from two opposite points of view—yes, *again*. Always and forever, I suppose.

I was approaching the situation subjectively, focusing on my feelings ("I feel like you don't like me when I'm that way"). Jack approached it objectively and factually ("I was trying to help you").

In the end, I had to accept the objective reality that he *was* trying to help me. But he also understood, and did not condemn, the way I was feeling about his reminders.

We tried to come up with a way he could help me when I get hyper without making me feel unaccepted, but we couldn't. In this case, I needed to *remember* and *accept* the way Jack does try to help me.

I want to be careful not to lump all women into the subjective, feeling-oriented category, although I suppose I would agree with some psychologists who believe that this feeling-oriented characteristic is true of more women than men. However, the need is to determine our individual pattern in approaching life and that of our partner. Then we must seek not only to understand and accept each way, but to complete each other as well.

My subjectiveness makes me overly sensitive to teasing, and I'll read into remarks implications that many times are not there. Another difficulty is that I have a little tape playing in my head of how I expect or want Jack to respond. If he doesn't respond according to my prerecorded version, the situation may be grossly misunderstood.

Before I began to study Jack's approach to life, I would buy a dress, bring it home, and ask, "How do you like my dress?"

If Jack's response was a simple "I like it," I'd take it back!

Why? Because Jack's "I like it" was too objective. He may have been stating a fact, but I was looking for an enthusiastic tone of voice, a raised eyebrow, a whistle—well, *something* to convey a sense of his approval.

We've really worked on this. Jack tries to express himself with more feeling, and I keep telling myself that he means what he says even when he's simply communicating an objective fact in plain, no-frills language.

Probably, a person who approaches life subjectively needs more reassurance—of all kinds—than does an objective person.

Being logical and objective, Jack has the MBTI types all catalogued and figured out (you may note that *he* wrote the appendix describing it). I'm still kind of fuzzy about some, but I'm trying. I must admit that I sometimes confuse these different characteristics. But as I've thought about it, these descriptions seem to be helpful:

■ Factual—looking at the facts.
■ Logical—the *process* of looking at the facts.
■ Objective—*outside* looking at the facts.

Using this as a guide, it would be possible for a subjective person who is *inside* and *feeling* a situation to still be logical and have a logical view of the facts.

But to be intuitive and objective might be harder.

To be emotional and objective is sort of tricky.

Emotional and factual? Well, maybe.

But to be subjective and factual, that would be tough!

And a factual and intuitive person—it seems as though that would be extremely difficult. (Did you get all that?)

Now that I've partially—or perhaps thoroughly!—confused you, let's go back and take another look.

According to studies done, many people are logical and organized who are also the feeling-type. In Myers-Briggs language they are SFs (Sensing/Feeling) people. In a book about using the various personality gifts for the good of the Body of Christ, pastor Gary Harbaugh gives an example:

> Where Mike (an ST) and Margie (an SF) differ is in how they prefer to make decisions. . . . Mike combines his Sensing way of looking at things with a Thinking (logical and analytical) way of making decisions. This ST combination results in a very special gift, the gift of realism and practicality, and the ability to focus on the here-and-now.
>
> Margie is also a present-oriented person, but she combines her Sensing way of perceiving with a different way of making decisions. She knows that it can be helpful to think through decisions logically and analytically, like Mike does, anticipating the consequences that will probably result from whatever action is taken today. However, when a really *significant* decision has to be made, Margie believes that logic cannot always be trusted. It may be the *logical* decision to make, but it may not *feel* right to her. Rather than rely on objective analysis, Margie's way of deciding is to base her decisions primarily on person-centered values. For her, cause and effect is spelled cause and *affect*: how will this particular decision affect people generally, and especially the important people in her life.
>
> Jung said that to decide with Feeling (F) is every bit as rational as to decide with Thinking. It is just that the *rationale* is

different. Mike makes the assumption that truth and fairness are fundamental to all choices, and his impersonal way of coming to a conclusion is not intended to be uncaring. On the contrary, Mike's *way* of caring is to make a decision as free as possible from personal bias.[1]

When I read that, a light clicked on!

In the past, when an organizational situation involving a special friend or relative needed attention, I'd push Jack to use his leadership position to get involved and change it for the better. But Jack seemed to lean over backwards to treat that situation in the same way he would approach any other person or situation, and he refused to be pushed. That would frustrate me because I thought he didn't care.

Now I understand that he *was caring* "by making a decision as free as possible from personal bias."

The combination of the intuitive but objective type person is rare. According to studies only about twenty percent of males and nine percent of females fit that category.[2] People with this combination tend to be intellectual, logical, and ingenious. They have a natural ability to do long-range planning and find problems stimulating. They are stimulated by complexity and enjoy seeing how everything fits together in patterns. Because they take feelings into consideration only when it is logical to do so, the intuitive-objective person can be misperceived as personally detached or even aloof. But their more impersonal approach to situations is not intended to be distant. It is, rather, the approach that a Thinking type believes will keep personal bias from getting in the way of the best resolution of a problem.[3]

Feeling types may find it hard to understand how they do it, but an intuitive-objective person can relatively easily separate a difference of opinion from personal feelings.[4]

So you see, there are all kinds of combinations of personality types and preferences and ways to make decisions.

But one thing seems clear to me: people usually marry their opposite.

Sometimes I long to be more objective. In certain situations, I've even worked hard at it! But it just doesn't last long. Soon I find myself involved up to my everlasting feelings and for the life of me, I can't stop being subjective.

According to the dictionary, *subjective* means something resulting from the feelings or temperament of the subject or person thinking. It is determined by and emphasizes the ideas, thoughts, and feelings of the artist or writer, not just rigidly transcribing or reflecting reality.

Picture Jack and me watching a presidential debate. I find it very difficult to watch, so I create all sorts of things to do to take me from the room. I find myself increasingly irritable—which unfortunately focuses on Jack a time or two.

Why is it hard for me to watch that debate? Because I get so personally involved! I wince when one attacks the other; when each seems to repeat information; when the other fumbles for a word. I hate the critical rehashing after the debate. The whole event makes me *sick*!

Jack can't figure out what's the matter with me. (And at first, I can't either!) Then I realize it's the same reason I can't stay in the room when Jack wants to watch a certain forum-type news program where the people on the program verbally attack each other, won't let the other finish sentences, and even call each other names! To me, it's horrible. To Jack, it's interesting.

Not *wrong*, my friends—just *different*.

Jack's objectivity views life one way, and my subjectivity fills out the picture.

Maturity is defined as being fully developed. As we grow mentally, spiritually, and emotionally, we will become more balanced people by *choosing* to learn the thinking and decision process of others who are different than we are. Author Gary Harbaugh puts it this way:

> Learning to develop and incorporate the differing gifts of others is not only a caring, Christian thing to do, it is also an *essential* thing to do for your own development as a whole person in Christ. In early life, our task is to recognize and develop God's special gifts to us so that we can be sure to use our gift effectively and faithfully "to equip the saints for the work of ministry, for building up the body of Christ" (Eph. 4:12). As we mature, however, and especially around mid-life and later, a deeper and more complete personal integration results from our becoming more comfortable with those gifts that are the opposite of our own. Becoming all that we are capable of being involves learning to incorporate those opposite gifts more and more

completely into our life. From this perspective, the efforts we make as Christians to appreciate and affirm those with gifts differing from our own can assist us in this personal growth toward wholeness.[5]

What's one of the best ways to learn this—and to grow into the mature person God wants you to be? Marry your opposite.

When two lives are rubbed together day after day, month after month, year after year, change should occur. We should grow. We should mature. We should become, as Rev. Harbaugh states, *whole*.

Is that one of the effects your marriage is having on *you*?

NOTES:

1. Gary L. Harbaugh, *God's Gifted People* (Minneapolis: Augsburg Publishing House, 1988), page 50.
2. Harbaugh, page 76.
3. Harbaugh, page 76.
4. Harbaugh, page 82.
5. Harbaugh, pages 47-48.

5

You See the Forest,
I See the Trees

CONCEPTUAL VS. DETAILED

CAROLE

Jack looked a bit grumpy as he came in that evening. I waited until he settled comfortably on the couch with his diet cola and the newspaper before I asked how the meeting had gone.

"Good," he said tersely.

"Then why do you look so grim?" I queried.

"Oh, I don't know," he responded and then paused. "Well, maybe I do. We spent most of the day listening to Dave's ideas, and they were really good, but it took him hours to *tell* us about them! He went into such great detail. . . ."

His voice trailed off. I quit asking questions and let him resume reading the evening paper.

Jack is a conceptual thinking. He has to work at listening to people who need to think out loud, go into details, bring up unrelated issues, and get off the subject. He does it, but it's hard for him.

Still, he *has* learned to do it—because that's exactly the way I am! I groove on details, want to hear *all* about them, and will spend hours telling—and listening to—all the intricacies of a situation.

One time our daughter Lynn and I spent fifteen minutes seriously discussing where we would pin a corsage on a type of dress that neither one of us had or intended to buy! As the discussion wound down, I laughed. When Lynn asked me what was funny, I said, "Can you imagine what Jack would think of this conversation?" She shrugged and rolled her eyes.

If a detail-minded person is not married to a person who loves to talk that way, then he or she needs to befriend another person (of the same sex) who does.

When Lynn left for college, I subconsciously tried to force Jack into being that person for me, and I lived in frustration for two months because he couldn't do it. I finally figured out what was causing my dilemma and began praying to find a woman who could be for me what Lynn had been up until then. But for a time there was no one, and I discovered a wonderful thing—God Himself could be that listening ear. I could "pour out [my heart] to him" (Psalm 62:8) in just the detailed way I needed to.

A number of women have complained to me that their husbands don't pray with them. And if they do, they don't pray "conversationally," which to these women means praying subject by subject, covering every small detail and conversing with the Lord about it. Some women even think their husbands lack spiritually because they don't like to pray in this way.

I love to pray with Jack. But when Jack and I pray together, we don't go back and forth conversationally. Jack prays and then I pray, or vice versa. For the most part he prays in concepts. He puts up the structure, and I fill in the cracks.

Again, this is not wrong. It is just different.

Most relationships need a great deal of give and take, of patience, of consideration. But that's what makes up love, isn't it?

It isn't that Jack never describes things in what I call the "Michener" form. Sometimes I am absolutely amazed as he gets carried away in lengthy description. But that is the exception and not the rule.

Before I began to understand that Jack thinks in concepts, not details, I spent many hours in tears.

In earlier years, Jack often attended week-long conferences while I stayed home with Lynn. When he arrived home, I'd wait eagerly for him to tell me *all* about the conference. So he'd tell me *all* about the conference—in ten minutes flat! I'd think, "He doesn't *care* enough to tell me about that conference. And if he doesn't care enough to tell me all about that conference, he must not *love* me the way I long to be loved."

I'd harbor that thought, retreat in my spirit, and often cry because I mistook a *difference* for a lack of his love.

It took me years to discover that because Jack zeroes in on the main concepts and the most important things, Jack *had,* in his way, told me *all* about that conference.

Then there would be the times I'd begin to tell him something—about our neighbor down the street, "the one whose uncle was a state senator . . . you know, his wife spent some time in a mental hospital when her boy got into drugs and he almost didn't make it through, especially when he was involved in an accident—it was Halloween and. . . ." About this time I'd notice that Jack's eyes were glazing over. I'd think, "He's not *listening*"—and I was right! Then my thoughts would proceed, "If he's not listening, then he's not interested in what I'm saying, and therefore he's not interested in *me*, and he must not *love* me the way I long to be loved"—and I was wrong!

What I didn't know about Jack's thinking processes could have filled a library.

Over the years, we've learned.

I can now condense a wonderful four-hour story down to ten minutes flat! But at other times, Jack understands that I've *just got to* tell him all the details. And he's trained himself to listen patiently. I love him for that.

On the other hand, he's learned to remember some of those really important details from a conference that I want to hear about. You know, like who got engaged, who's going to have a baby, the best meal he had—some of those vital things!

We're getting there. (Only a bottom-liner will ask me *where*.)

Dr. H. Norman Wright calls this "learning to speak the language" of your spouse. I call it learning to adjust to the way your loved one thinks and talks.

But whatever you title this difference, it is a vital one to understand.

And adjust to.

And compromise with.

And yes, even learn to love.

If you don't, it will *drive you crazy!*

6

Are You Listening?
THE KEY TO UNDERSTANDING

JACK

"No position in life offers more chance for advancement and maturity than marriage," states John Drescher, "yet here we are most afraid to face ourselves." He goes on to say:

> Who knows you better, your weaknesses and strengths, than the person to whom you are married? Who is more interested in making you a better person than the one whose very life depends on you? What better sounding board could you find to test your thoughts, ideas and plans?
>
> There is a great blessing in learning how to complement one another. First, we need to really listen to what the other is saying; to forget ourselves, to try to understand the other's point of view. We must be willing to say, "I know I may not think or act like you, but I will try to understand how you feel about this."[1]

Mr. Drescher is right in urging us to see the world through the other's eyes.

"Deep sharing is overwhelming, and very rare," writes Paul Tournier. "A thousand fears keep us in check. First of all there is the fear of breaking down, of crying. There is especially the fear that the other will not sense the tremendous importance with which this memory or feeling is charged. How painful it is when such a difficult sharing falls flat, upon ears either preoccupied or mocking, ears in any case that do not sense the significance of what we're saying."[2]

Another experienced counselor was asked, "What is the essential characteristic of a happy marriage?"

"After love," he replied, "the ability to confide fully, freely, and frankly in each other."

Over and over from many voices comes the crying need to *listen* to each other . . . to *hear in depth.*

They were a handsome couple—young, well-educated, intense. However, they weren't looking their best at the moment. Her eyes were brittle-bright, exposing a nervousness that skittered across the luncheon table. He looked drawn and tired.

We had been surprised to hear of their permanent return to the States from one of the most difficult mission fields in the world. But even more surprising was their story.

The reasons were multiple, of course. But one fact stood out. The wife had had reservations from the beginning about going overseas, and had expressed these to her husband—but *he had not listened.*

A friend of ours had a character trait that caused him to filter and distort information. It eventually hindered his effectiveness in leadership. For years his wife had tried to help him with this tendency. But *he had not listened.*

God leads two people together so one can compensate for the other's weaknesses. If we are not listening to the person who loves us the most, has our best interests at heart, and is in the best position to see our faults, sins, and inadequacies, then we can be weakened by several deficiencies.

First, we will not be "sharpened" by that relationship as God intended.

Second, our prayers could be hindered. Peter cautions husbands in 1 Peter 3:7: "Husbands, in the same way be considerate as you live with your wives, and treat them with respect as the weaker partner and as heirs with you of the gracious gift of life, so that nothing will hinder your prayers." In verse 8 he sums up by exhorting "all" to be harmonious, sympathetic, loving, kind-hearted, and humble. How can our married lives be harmonious and kind, how can we be truly understanding, if we do not *listen* to our partner? And if we are not understanding, God says our very communication with Him might be hindered.

And third, we might end up a nervous wreck! Amos 3:3 says, "Can two walk together, except they be agreed?" (KJV). Living with someone twenty-four hours a day who disagrees with you about important issues will affect your physical, mental, or emotional health.

Finally, we may miss out on the complete will of God for our lives.

If we are listening in order to understand—or *heart-hearing*—we will be able to put ourselves in the other's shoes and take into serious consideration that person's thoughts and feelings in making decisions. Tragically, some Christian men feel that if they have simply listened to their wife's words, then they have adequately considered her viewpoint. Then they go ahead and make decisions independently.

Listening, according to *Webster,* means "to make a conscious effort to hear; attend closely"; but the second meaning is, "to give heed; take advice."

God calls us to be one in marriage. Some husbands know that, but somehow think *they* are the "one." Oneness means a lot of things, but certainly it means to be intertwined both in heart and in mind. Therefore, agreement on major decisions is essential before action is taken.

Some men may be thinking, "But then my wife could hold me back from doing what I feel God wants me to do."

God's commands do not contradict each other. God calls us to be "one flesh," to be subject to one another, to love, to prefer, to look out for the best interest of our mate. How can this be done when we take the attitude, "Well, thanks for your opinion. Now I'll do what I want to do"—or even "what I think God wants."

This area seems paradoxical. How can God ordain or

opposite minds? What *should* be our approach on major

ke the case of the first couple I mentioned. The husband felt called to a tough and formidable mission field. His wife didn't feel that she had either the gifts or the capacity for it, but he refused to consider a less demanding country. When he didn't heed her feelings, she went with him as wholeheartedly as she was able because she wanted to support him. Two years later they were back home, the wife near a breakdown, the husband defeated.

I believe that prayer is the answer. Not the ordinary, send-up-a-word kind of prayer, but agonizing, time-consuming, fervent prayer. *Until.* Until God reaches down and fills that wife's heart with His call to the same field and gives her the gifts and abilities to live there with joy. Or until the husband's heart is changed to stay home contentedly or redirected to a less difficult field of service.

But because this husband had not listened to his wife, he *didn't* pray until God changed her or the situation. And as a result, two people were deeply hurt.

To love is to listen, and God says three times in one chapter (Ephesians 5) "Husbands *love* your wives."

But listening with one's heart is only the first step. The second is to learn how to express what we are thinking and feeling in a way our spouse can understand. This is probably one of the most difficult tasks we face in marriage because we feel that *of course* our partners ought to reason the way we reason. We assume that if we are patient, communicate well, pray together (or perhaps even cajole, urge, nag, be adamant, push, pout, and get angry), then *someday* in our years of marriage, we will think alike.

Wrong!

You may come together on your viewpoints, likes and dislikes, preferences in travel, and how money should be spent, but you will never think alike. In fact, thinking alike isn't even the goal. As someone has said, "If two people think alike, one of them is unnecessary."

Thinking *together* is the goal—bringing our thoughts to each other time after time in *understanding* the other's reasoning.

Understand, for instance, that intuitive, feeling people . . .

■ may take criticism of their ideas more personally than was intended. So take their feelings into account when telling them something.

- do not take teasing well—they'll take it personally every time!
- tend to overcommit themselves because it's hard for them to say no—especially when someone needs help.

Understand, too, that factual, objective people . . .

- need more understanding and support in the *emotional* area because the feeling side of life tends to be less familiar to them.
- will talk more about what they are *doing* or *thinking* than how they are *feeling* and may neglect to ask other people about how they are feeling.
- may show love more by doing things than by talking deeply.
- are often linear learners and will appreciate being led through a topic step by step.

Understand, particularly, that the best decisions are those made together by one objective, logical person and one subjective, feeling person. Those decisions will be thought-through, realistic, and relevant, but they will consider the people who will be affected.

Yet still another step is necessary. After understanding, our goal is to learn how to balance and complete the strengths and weaknesses we see in us as a couple.

As you are well aware by now, Carole and I are vastly different. We *contrast* the way we think in almost everything, such as:

- the way we *plan.*
  - Carole usually plans when she's in the mood to think about something.
  - I plan based on what needs to be worked on at the moment, whether or not I'm in the mood.
- in our *work habits.*
  - Carole just *begins* without much planning for what needs to be done, or without organizing the work in proper sequence. She sees something to be done, and she *does* it—the fastest and easiest way possible.
  - I'm slower, more careful. I prepare before starting to make sure that first I have everything I need.
- in the way we *organize.*
  - Carole is inclined to do it the easy, more hassle-free way.
  - I'm inclined to do research, think, get more facts, try to make the best and most logical choice.

Let me stop here a minute lest you think I'm putting down Carole's way. A lot of the time the way she does it makes great sense. For instance, not long ago, we observed an old car—I mean a *very* old car—obviously in the middle of renovation. The owner had spent many hours already trying to strip the paint off it but had succeeded only in clearing a few small sections. He was using time he didn't have, the car wasn't going to look like much even when he finished, and he was discouraged. Carole looked it over and said, "Are you sure you want to go to all that work? Being a non-perfectionist, I'd just spray-paint over the whole thing. But then," she added quickly, "you probably couldn't live with that."

The man looked startled and then grinned. "Yes, I guess I could. In fact, I'll do that tomorrow." And he did. In this case her *fast* way was the best way in the light of time spent for something not worth it.

- in the way we *play and use leisure time.*
  - Carole is a sightseer, a looker, but adventuresome in wanting to try new things.
  - I tend to be a nonparticipant (except in certain sports) not inclined to try new things.
- in the way we *give.*
  - Carole is a spontaneous, impulsive, generous giver.
  - I am a measured, thoughtful, planned giver.
- in our thinking as it regards *spending time with people.*
  - I'm inclined to review time with people in the light of what is accomplished.
  - Just being with people accomplishes the objective for Carole.

How can we balance and complete each other when we come at life with such significant differences?

I can't tell *you* the specifics of how to do it, because each couple is unique, created by God in different ways. But let me throw out some ideas.

Primary is the need to accept and not try to change the way your partner thinks and responds to life.

Our fun is increased because of Carole's imaginative mind, but the background for those times is well-planned because of the way I think. I assist her to think things through and to set goals. She aids me in relaxing and enjoying life more.

With many couples, the very differences that *attracted* become sources for *attack.* How can we reverse this process?

Try this on for size: Take a weekend, or at least a full day, just for the two of you. Enjoy a wonderful breakfast out and then find a place where you can be alone.

First, pray together about your time, and then separate for an hour. During that hour, pray, read the Word, and talk over with the Lord what your goals should be for the next month, the next six months—maybe even for a year. Make these concrete, measurable goals. (Remember: A goal is something you have control over. A desire is something you'd like to see happen but can't make happen. For instance, you desire that your children be godly. You pray for it. But that can't be a goal because you are not able to control their wills or responses. Your goal might be to teach them a Bible verse each week or to pray for them each day.)

After that hour, get together and share the goals (personal, marriage, family, ministry can all be worked on, but stick to marriage goals for this time), combine them, set some activities that will accomplish those goals along with the scheduled time to do them. Then bring them to the Lord together.

Now, take the rest of the day to enjoy each other!

Any couple who did this every three months or so would make a tremendous beginning toward balancing and completing the way they think.

To review:

- *Listen* with your heart.
- *Communicate* until you understand.
- Grow in *understanding* until you accept.
- Continue *accepting* until you can affirm.
- *Affirm* until you can grow in the strengths of the other.
- Periodically *set goals* for your marriage and review them.

And may one of the topics, for both goal-setting and communication, be the question, "How can we begin to work on using our differences to be *assets* in our marriage rather than *liabilities*? What practical things can we do to make them possibilities rather than problems?"

Difficult? You bet!

Exciting? Definitely.

And, my friends, *time worth spending*.

Now—just do it!

NOTES:
1. John Drescher, "Formula for a Happy Marriage," *Christian Life* (July 1970), page 28.
2. Paul Tournier, *To Understand Each Other* (Atlanta: John Knox Press, 1967), pages 28-29.

PART II

THE WAY WE RELATE

You Say Goodbye, I Say Hello

INTROVERT VS. EXTROVERT

CAROLE

As the wedding processional ended, the ushers began dismissing the guests by rows. We stood to go through the reception line when Jack leaned close to me and whispered, "Let's skip the reception."

I smiled cheerfully and said, "Maybe we'll be able to duck out after thirty minutes or so."

Years ago, I would have either (1) groaned at his suggestion, (2) decided that Jack was an unsociable lout, (3) agreed to duck out and then felt cheated the rest of the day, or (4) insisted on staying while feeling put out that he'd even suggested leaving.

But now, I understand him better.

He is sociable. He isn't a lout. He doesn't hate people. It's just that he is an introvert.

Many people in the United States feel that being introverted is undesirable. One family counselor we know says that in his opinion there are a lot of "closet introverts" living in the United States. They think being an introvert is socially unacceptable so they try to cover up by working hard at what they assume *is* acceptable.

On the other hand, seventy-five percent of Orientals test out as introverts—apparently more socially acceptable in Asia. But it's my guess that people around the world are about fifty-fifty in the extrovert/introvert factor.

What comes to your mind when you hear the word *introvert*? Is it a picture of a person who doesn't like to be with people, who is solitary, reclusive, unsociable, and silent?

Let's dispense with that image once and for all. In reality, an introvert is a person who is energized by inner resources and internal experience; one who reflects and then (maybe) acts.

An extrovert, on the other hand, is one who is energized by other people and external experiences; one who acts, then (maybe) reflects.[1]

Now it *is* true that an introvert is often reserved, quiet, and perhaps difficult to know. Introverts may bottle up and guard their emotions. They do need privacy and time alone, and some could seem withdrawn to extroverts. But one of their great contributions is that they give life *depth*. They *think* before they speak. They reflect and contemplate. The introvert is liable to be the poet, the philosopher, the theologian.

The extrovert, on the other hand, may be talkative, friendly, and easy to know. Extroverts express emotions more readily and need relationships to a greater extent. Extroverts give *breadth* to life. However, extroverts may seem shallow or superficial to introverts.[2]

Both attitudes are used by everyone at times—extroverts want time alone, introverts want time with people—but one is usually more dominant.

Jack and I like these positive definitions. They have helped us discover not only who we are, but why we respond to certain situations the way we do.

Someone has said that youth is the time to discover who you are, and middle age is the time to develop the other part of who you are. This seems particularly necessary with the extrovert and introvert tendencies. I think the Lord Jesus in His humanity had the *perfect balance* of both.

The older Jack and I get, the closer together we grow on this one. Each of us has helped the other to draw on some of the good qualities of the external and internal strengths. Jack has taught me the value of solitude, and now I seek more time alone than I did in my twenties. I realize that not only do I want more time with God—to study Him, to know Him, to talk with Him, to reflect about Him—but I need more time just to separate myself and sit quietly. When I have time alone, my creative juices start to flow. I also experience recuperation, times of storing up and becoming replenished for extended times with people.

Jack has developed a greater capacity for people in social and ministry situations, but I continue to have greater ability to be with people more hours and more days. I can go from ten to fourteen days without feeling as though someone unscrewed my big toe and drained away all the energy, but after three or four days Jack needs an evening or a day to himself. We now take this into consideration in planning any kind of trip. But the plus side of completing each other and adjusting to each other in this area is that while I am *able* to go longer relating to people, I start to run on sheer nervous energy without realizing it. So taking more frequent breaks for Jack's needs helps me to keep my energy reserves full.

Another implication of our differences in this area is in our conversation with other couples and with groups. I not only tend to act and then reflect, but to *speak* and then reflect. Jack, on the other hand, reflects and then speaks.

Now this can be a problem! I can spout off ten sentences in answer to a question before Jack opens his mouth! But if I can control my tongue and hold back my surface answer, Jack will speak—and present deep truth! I have to confess, I squirm and struggle on this one. But when I do watch my speech, our conversation has much more depth than when I go on and on about nothing.

On the other hand, when it comes to small talk, which Jack can only take about seven minutes of, he *counts* on me to carry the conversation for both of us.

A great many extroverts think out loud because hearing themselves say things to other people helps them to better clarify their own understanding. An introvert, however, often keeps his thinking process inside—reflecting, weighing, considering—and only when a conclusion has been reached is he ready to share his thoughts out loud with others.

But talkative and outgoing people are not all extroverts. Our granddaughter, Sonya, has taught us this. Sonya's nickname is Sunny—and she lives up to that name. She has a quick smile, a generally exuberant personality, and an outgoing nature. In most social situations, she seems at ease. Yet we are convinced Sunny is an introvert. Why? Because Sunny needs time to soak up aloneness as much as she needs air to breathe. If she doesn't get time to be by herself, she gets cranky. She can play by the hour with her dolls, make up games, pretend. Now of course, part of that is a God-given imagination that she uses actively. But part of it is her need for solitude. Outgoing, but an introvert—at least by the above positive definition.

On the other hand, our grandson, Eric, is an extrovert though he is more naturally quiet and not quite so at ease in every situation. Even when he was very little, he wanted company. Not for him were hours of playing by himself. No, he wanted someone to play a game *with him*, to read *to* him, to be *together*.

Both are social creatures. Both converse freely with adults. But Sunny is energized by internal experiences and inner resources, and Eric by people, sports, and external experiences.

What we must remember is that these are two complementary attitudes toward the world. One is not "better" than the other.

Have you ever met a professor who was a marvelous conversationalist who could converse on any number of topics—and then would leave the group after a few minutes to hide in the library with a good book? He is probably an introvert.

We went to school with a man who is now one of the most sought-after speakers in the country, known for his brilliant wit. We had this man and his wife over for a barbecue along with a few other couples. Although he contributed to the conversation, he was one of the most silent members of the group. I think I could have guessed it—because his teaching is deep and reflective—he is no doubt an introvert.

This characteristic needs to be met head-on, understood, and then *appreciated*. But, boy, it took us a while.

Much of life is affected by these tendencies in areas such as:

Vacations. The extrovert loves tours, wants to see family and friends, prefers the big hotel scene, crowds, galas, reunions, celebrations of all kinds.

The introvert probably wants to retreat from most of those things. He loves hiking, exploring ancient cities, back-country camping, fishing, small hotels or condos.

Entertaining and social gatherings. Capacity is one factor here but another may be the desire of the introvert to relate to a few (one to four) deeply rather than many casually. Jack will tend to single out one person and have an in-depth discussion rather than go from group to group. The extrovert loves, or at least doesn't mind, the big dinner parties, wedding receptions, potluck suppers at the church, various kinds of get-togethers.

Number of friends and acquaintances. Extroverts usually have a greater number of people with whom they want to stay in touch but introverts will often have significantly more depth in their (fewer) relationships.

Even as I write this, I realize how Jack and I have meshed on these different preferences—for our greater enjoyment, I believe. Neither of us prefers the big hotel, but we choose to stay at a condo or cabin where we can relax and at least cook our own breakfast without having to venture into a dining room. We usually prefer to relate to just one another on vacations, perhaps because much of our time in our job is spent with people. So we pick the smaller accommodations and the smaller groups to entertain.

However, Jack still wants to skip the wedding reception while I desire to stay and visit with guests; I'm inclined to talk longer into the night when we are staying with a family; I'll volunteer to join the "party" if there's anything going on that looks interesting; I still want to have a huge group at Thanksgiving (and Jack humors me in that).

The manner in which Jack and I get up in the morning is a microcosm of our tendencies. Usually, Jack gets up earlier than I do, slips quietly out of the bedroom, goes downstairs and pops a cup of coffee (carefully left from the day before) into the microwave while he brews a fresh pot. Then he sits down on the sofa to pray, to think, to *sit*. After a bit, he gets more coffee, goes up to his study, closes the door, and has his time with the Lord.

When I get up thirty minutes later, I'm going before I hit the floor. I make the bed, do my exercises, put on my makeup, dress, and then come down for a cup of coffee to take up with me when I have my time with God. While the coffee is heating in the microwave, I clean up anything that needs to be put away in the kitchen.

Where do you belong in the extrovert/introvert categories? Take a look at these descriptors:

Let's Identify

KEY WORDS[3]

Extroversion	Introversion
Active	Reflective
Outward	Inward
Sociable	Reserved
People	Privacy
Many	Few
Breadth	Depth
Expressive	Quiet

In addition, extroverts like action and variety; enjoy doing mental work by talking to people; act quickly, sometimes without much reflection; and want to know what other people expect. Introverts like quiet and time to consider things; prefer to do mental work privately before talking; may be slow to try something without understanding it; and want to set their own standards.[4]

Family counselor Dr. Gary Oliver uses a helpful illustration in his workshops that crystallizes the definitions of this pair of opposites: for the introvert, "the unexamined life is not worth living"; for the extrovert, "the unlived life is not worth examining."

I really hope you aren't like your spouse in this one!

William J. Petersen, in writing of missionaries Adoniram and Ann (Nancy) Hasseltine Judson, tells of their remarkable compatibility despite extreme differences. She was fun-loving, spoiled, impetuous, stubborn, social. Friends said that no one could be gloomy or unhappy around her. Sound like an extrovert?

Adoniram was brilliant, sometimes moody, and a bit eccentric—and from childhood preferred books to play. Introvert, right?

They married and set sail for India aboard a wretched ship which Nancy described as looking like Noah's ark. But after confessing her apprehensions of dying at sea, she began to enjoy the voyage. To get exercise, Adoniram and Nancy skipped rope and danced!

I laughed out loud when I read that! Imagine that serious-minded bookworm dancing on board a crowded ship! That was Nancy's contribution to his health and welfare.

They endured incredible hardship in taking the Gospel to India and

Burma: their first child was stillborn; her health was poor; the work was slow, hard, and lonely; they had no American friends; letters from home took years; their second boy died at eight months of age; Adoniram was put into prison and Nancy lived in a nearby room to help him. But, as Mr. Petersen writes, their marriage was a success. They "respected and honored each other, despite their idiosyncrasies. Though they often worked as a team, each gave the other space to develop independently. They had no better friends than each other."[5]

Perhaps that's part of the secret of a marriage joining extrovert to introvert: giving each other space to develop, to be a team, to learn what it means to be best friends.

When I become silent, Jack thinks I'm either sick, angry, or near death. (Though now he knows there *are* times when I really don't feel like talking!) I take after my mother on this one. I can still hear Dad saying, "When I'm with your mother, I don't need a radio." Then, with a slow smile, he'd add, "I talk in my sleep because it's the only way I can get a word in edgewise." But his words carried no malice. He adored Mother.

Because these differences affect so many situations in life, a great deal of compromise is necessary to adjust to them such as staying a limited time at a party, taking work to do so the other can get needed time alone on a trip, or maintaining separate relationships that don't involve the other. Giving each other space is needed as well.

But above all, the extrovert and introvert personalities must be *understood* and *accepted*—in order to love. In order to grow in marriage.

In order to be—as you desire to be—*best friends*.

NOTES:
1. Earle C. Page, *Looking At Type* (Gainesville, FL: C.A.P.T., 1983).
2. From a seminar on the MBTI by Dr. Gary Oliver.
3. Page, *Looking At Type*.
4. Gary L. Harbaugh, *God's Gifted People* (Minneapolis: Augsburg Publishing House, 1988), page 23.
5. William J. Petersen, "Vows That Beat All Odds," *Partnership* (September-October 1987), page 47.

8

You Say Stop, I Say Go
ORGANIZED VS. FREE SPIRIT

CAROLE

The sun was warm on my face. The ice clinked musically as we swirled our diet colas around in the glasses. The small deck of the condo where we were enjoying a three-day break in our schedule looked out on a green fairway, and we lazily watched some golfers take their shots. I sighed in contentment and then continued perusing the resort magazine.

"Wow! Look at this!" I exclaimed. "We can go on a three hour white-water rafting trip tomorrow morning at eight. What do you think about that?"

A few years ago, Jack would have groaned, but now only a small sigh escaped him. There was a moment of quiet and then he countered, "Wouldn't you just as soon rent a couple of bikes and ride around this place?"

"No, I really wouldn't," I declared. "But if white-water rafting sounds awful to you, I guess I'll settle for bicycling."

He grinned. "No, if you really want to go rafting, let's do it."

A few minutes later, we walked over to the resort village and purchased our tickets for the raft trip.

The next morning we swooshed down the river, got soaking wet, and *had a ball!*

At the end of the morning, Jack said (not even grudgingly, mind you), "I'm glad you talked me into that. It was great."

Over the years, we've been both exasperated and thankful for our different approaches to planning.

When Jack and I took the Myers-Briggs Type Indicator, we found that we were similar in only one area—but even in that one, we are poles apart in actuality.

The area in which we came the closest was what the MBTI calls *judging* and *perception*. The judging attitude is one that prefers an organized lifestyle, likes definite order and structure, and likes to have life under control. That person enjoys being decisive and likes clear limits and categories.

The perceptive attitude prefers a flexible lifestyle, likes going with the flow, prefers to experience life as it happens, enjoys being curious and discovering surprises. That person likes freedom to explore without limits.

The MBTI suggests that the key word for *judging* is *closure*, and the key word for *perception* is *openness*. It proposes that judgers may seem demanding, rigid, and uptight to perceptives; but perceptives may seem disorganized, messy (fast), and irresponsible to judgers.

To me the titles *judging* and *perceptive* are confusing because I think of a *judging* person as someone who judges others, and that isn't what this means at all.

So let's change the names and call these two types the *organized* and the *free spirit*.

Jack and I were startled to find that in the MBTI, we *both* were on the "organized" side of the scale (we knew *he* would be!), although Jack tested out much stronger in this area than I did. But I learned something about myself as well, because as I reflected, I realized that I *do* like to plan my days. Some of the time, I want firm reservations, known schedules, and goals laid out.

But I prefer to have my goals only in my head and not on paper the way Jack does, and I don't want to be held to them too firmly. I love "scheduled unscheduled" Saturdays where we have a vague idea of what we want to do but are free to follow our inclinations. And I love being surprised by the unexpected pleasures. (Of course, Jack does too!)

So, although I am on the organized side of the scale in some things,

I hop over into the "free spirit" category quite often.

Jack is a much more firmly entrenched structured person.

And that's okay. Organized people need free spirits for fun in their lives, and free spirits desperately need organized persons to help get tasks done. This has been a difference we have thoroughly enjoyed adjusting to (well, for the most part) right from the beginning.

But it isn't the case with everyone. And of course, some people are not only extreme to one degree or the other, but refuse to learn and change as they grow older.

A friend of ours told us about meeting a recently retired military officer at the spectacular Hearst estate in California. The officer and his wife were on a ninety-day vacation, but they were behind schedule and couldn't spend much time looking at San Simeon. Our friend found out that this man had planned every *minute* of those ninety days—from exactly how many miles he and his wife were going to travel each day to every single attraction they were going to see. He had ninety nights' worth of reservations made in advance. A few days into the vacation, he and his wife were already exhausted.

Here was an extreme structurer! He reminded me of the man I read about who drove up to a viewing point at the Grand Canyon, told his family to stay in the car, rushed over and took pictures, sped back to the car, and said, "Let's go! We'll look at the pictures later."

And then there's my friend who declared emphatically, "I will *never* help him with planning a camp again! It was a *disaster*. He left everything to the last minute, informed me the morning it was to begin that I'd have to be in charge of the music, he hadn't detailed the program . . ." and on and on she steamed. When she finally groaned to a stop, her wheels locked as she repeated, "*Never again!*"

It wasn't hard to see what had happened. Her husband prided himself on being the free-spirit type, and it wasn't for him to be imprisoned in details of advance planning.

I suspect that an organized female "J" married to the free-spirited male "P" can be an especially sensitive and complex union that will demand much adjusting. He dreams, she analyzes. He envisions a trip, she pays the bills. He has a visionary plan, she cowers at the consequences.

We know several couples where the wife is the organizer and the husband is a real free spirit. In one case, a husband invited numerous relatives to their very small vacation cabin for several days. When his wife asked, "Where will everyone sleep?" his response was, "Oh, it'll work out. Everyone can just grab a bed." (His wife knew that would be like playing musical chairs. Fortunately, she got involved in the sleeping accommodations before everyone arrived.)

Free spirits are not usually adept at planning ahead and take the "It'll all work out" attitude. They often fly by the seat of their pants and may object to *any* scheduling, feeling it will take the fun out of life. On the other hand, highly organized persons have a difficult time with changes of plans—especially last-minute changes. Their minds simply don't adjust well.

We need to learn from each other on this one. If true free spirits don't want to drive organized people right up a wall, they'd better do some work on changing. And if highly organized people—like that retired military officer—don't want to have one unhappy spouse, they'd better learn to relax a bit! (Actually, that man did relent when he became so tired, and he did the "unthinkable"—he cancelled every single reservation and decided to go one day at a time. We say, "Yea for him!")

Remember, the name of the game is *change*, as well as *understand*. By "change," we mean not becoming *like* the other, but rather developing in appreciation for, and in some aspects of, the opposite preference of the other person.

But there is so much to appreciate about the differences in this area. Free spirits may be willing to step out and take needed chances in a new business; they may add creativity to a home; urge the family to make a needed change; or have a greater propensity to trust God and receive special instruction from the Lord. But they need the stability of their opposites to guard against deceptive voices or foolish ideas.

Jack admits he could be a kind of humdrum person if he were married to an extremely organized wife. He would be inclined to ignore exploring the castles, driving the dune buggies, shooting the rapids.

I appreciate Jack—and need him too. He untangles my life when I take on too much, helps me with priorities and goals, and encourages me to accomplish my dreams.

Let's Identify

KEY WORDS[1]

Organized	*Free Spirit*
Judgment	Perception
Organized	Flexible
Structure	Flow
Control	Experience
Decisive	Curious
Deliberate	Spontaneous
Closure	Openness
Plan	Wait
Deadlines	Discoveries
Productive	Receptive

Now let's identify who we are a bit more. Which answer better describes how you usually feel or act?

1. When you go somewhere for the day, would you rather . . .
   a. plan what you will do and when, or
   b. just go?
2. Do you prefer to . . .
   a. arrange dates, parties, etc., well in advance, or
   b. be free to do whatever looks like fun when the time comes?
3. Does the idea of making a list of what you should get done over the weekend . . .
   a. appeal to you,
   b. leave you cold, or
   c. positively depress you?
4. When it is settled well in advance that you will do a certain thing at a certain time, do you find it . . .
   a. nice to be able to plan accordingly, or
   b. a little unpleasant to be tied down?

Organized persons want to get decisions out of the way. They consider what needs to be done and make the appropriate decision, which puts closure on an area and makes it possible for them to get on with the rest of life. But for free spirits, making a final decision may close off options and opportunities or keep them from leaving the door open for new possibilities.

I hopped over to the free-spirit side of me recently and saw this difference in living color.

Our daughter, her husband, and our two grandchildren, who live in Mexico, came to Colorado Springs for a year. We had the joy of house-hunting for them so they would have a place to move into upon arrival.

We saw a home that met all their requirements early in our search but I kept saying, "Well, let's look a little more. Maybe we'll find something that goes Boong."

Jack was patient and looked with me for about three more weeks. Then he said, "Honey, I'd like to settle it *this weekend*."

We settled on that very first home we looked at, which really did have more going for it than any of the others. (But I would have looked some more. . . .)

I don't think Jack thinks of me as being indecisive—though some organized people would. But I probably try his patience at times when I want to "think about it later."

But let me remind you once again one thing we learned from the Myers-Briggs: Almost everyone jumps back and forth between the organized approach and the free-spirit approach, but one is usually preferred.

Have you figured out your own preferred attitude? Your partner's? If so, take fifteen minutes to sit down and think about:

- what frustrates you about the difference.
- what are the positive aspects of the differences.
- how God can use them.

Now pray through the lists.

Every time I do this, I come up with new things to appreciate in Jack. You will be able to discover some in your partner as well.

God will show us how to compensate for each other's weaknesses. We need to cry from our hearts the psalmist's prayer in Psalm 139: "Search me, O God, and know my heart; test me and know my anxious thoughts. See if there is any offensive way in me, and lead me in the way everlasting." The Lord will show us what needs to be changed in each of us and will give us the grace to accept what can't or shouldn't be changed in our mates.

And yes, this does take work. *Hard* work. But the rewards are fantastic!

Let's determine to knuckle down and mentally perspire as we give ourselves to this task of . . .

knowing,
understanding,
appreciating,
and then . . . changing.
May God Himself give us help.
We surely need it!

NOTE:

1. Adapted by Dr. Gary Oliver, from *Looking At Type*, by Earle C. Page (Gainesville, FL: C.A.P.T., 1983).

9

The Question
of Romance

AFFECTIONATE VS. RESERVED

JACK

One day a few years into our marriage, Carole let me know that we needed to have a Big Discussion. You know the kind. No little spur-of-the-moment verbal exchange, but a Serious Talk. I tend to want to delay these as long as possible, but I'd learned by then that this was not wise.

The conversation went something like this:

"You know, sweetheart," Carole began, "I'm beginning to wonder about something. It seems to me that usually I'm the one to initiate touching, hugging, kissing—that kind of affection. And I've had the growing feeling that this is not something you enjoy. Sometimes you appear almost embarrassed by it. Other times, you seem to brush it away and merely stand there."

She paused, trying to choose her words carefully. "I know that touching and affection are not necessarily barometers of love, and I know you love me. But I don't want to be doing something that you don't like or that embarrasses you. I have to admit, touching is important to me, but I want to please you and I will try to change in this area if you want me to."

CAROLE

He makes it sound much more controlled than I remember it! I cried buckets of tears over this, and prayed, and cried some more. Then I pleaded for God's wisdom and, punctuated with pauses to wipe my eyes, the Serious Talk began.

JACK

I swallowed. What she said was true. At times when I came home, she would greet me with an exuberant hug and kiss and I'd just stand there like a telephone pole. Apparently, Carole had gotten tired of hugging a telephone pole.

I was brought up in a home in which love was not expressed with a lot of hugging and kissing—although I knew my parents loved me. Carole's home was just the opposite. The usual way of saying "thanks" or "you're great" or "I love you" was a big bear hug and a kiss. Often touchers and non-touchers end up married to one another.

However, my reserve wasn't simply a product of my family background. I tend to be more restrained in expressing *any* emotion, not just affection. It isn't that I don't have strong emotions, I just don't wear them in public.

It didn't take me long to realize what my response should be on this one, however. You see, I *liked* the affectionate nature of my wife. I enjoyed her touches, hugs, and kisses. So I said, "Honey, I'm sorry you have felt that I don't like your affection. I'll have to admit, because of my background and nature, I am a bit embarrassed at times—when you kiss me in public or in front of company. But I like it! So please don't change. Don't stop."

I knew that I needed to go still one more step, and so I added, "In fact, I want to learn to be more affectionate toward you—to be at ease in expressing emotion—even in public. So be patient with me and help me learn."

And she was and did. She became my hugging and kissing coach (and I was an apt pupil). Now, after all these years, I can hug and kiss with the best of them!

The more we read and study and have experienced life, the more I am grateful that God helped me to be willing to change. I no longer feel awkward in some of the social situations in which we find ourselves. I don't feel ill at ease when the culture of a country demands a hug and a kiss on both cheeks—when you come *and* when you go—or with hostesses who expect a hug upon arrival. Touching has become a part of me and a part of growing.

Carole and I see increasing evidence of the great need that most humans have just to be touched. In *Love Life for Every Married Couple*, Dr. Ed Wheat states,

> God created us with hundreds of thousands of microscopic nerve endings in our skin designed to sense and benefit from a loving touch. A tender touch tells us that we are cared for. It can calm our fears, soothe pain, bring us comfort, or give us the blessed satisfaction of emotional security. As adults, touching continues to be a primary means of communicating with those we love, whether we are conscious of it or not. Our need for a caring touch is normal and healthy and we will never outgrow it. . . . Physical contact is absolutely essential in building the emotion of love. You may take it as a sobering warning that most of the time marital infidelity is not so much a search for sex as it is for emotional intimacy.[1]

Just recently Carole and I talked to a couple where the man said, "I need more affection. She doesn't *touch* me or seem to have a need to be touched. I long for more physical touching, hugs, and kisses."

There was more going on in this marriage than lack of affection on the wife's part, and we discovered some reasons why she was pulling away from her husband, but here was a *wife* who needed to work on being outwardly demonstrative and affectionate.

Mostly, however, it seems women have the greater desire for more nonsexual touching, for tenderness, for romance.

In a cartoon by Lynn Johnson, a wife asks her husband (who, his back toward her, is resting on the couch), "Do you take me for granted, John? Have we been married so long that the passion has gone out of our relationship?" By this time he is sitting up sleepily on the couch, and she's shaking him. "Do you look at me with the same sense of longing that you had when we first fell in love?"

The last frame shows him staggering away saying, "Wait. I'll get my glasses."[2]

A reader wrote to a national magazine with the question, "Is romance dead after marriage?" She went on to say that, in her experience and most of her friends' experience, there is no romance left after several years of marriage. She missed those warm feelings. "There is a very special part of women that periodically requires the nourishment of romance," she wrote.

The writer of the article wisely called this reader and several of her friends *and their husbands* for a conference. While the women were in one room complaining about the lack of romance in their lives, the men were in another saying things like:

It's something I want as much as she does. Listen—before we were married I used to get all kinds of indications from her that I was recognized as somebody special, that I was wanted. The fact that we're married now doesn't mean that I'm willing to take that for granted. I still want those signals from her that say she wants me and finds me exciting.

One ponytailed mother of two young children, sitting cross-legged on the floor, tried to tell why she felt so good about her marriage. "He confirms me as a woman," she explains, "and I think I confirm him as a man."

The author said, "Is that what romance is all about? Is that why it's so important to feel actively desired and consciously pursued? Seen in those terms, romance is far more than the lost giddiness of courtship. It is that completed sense of our womanliness, that fulfillment of our sexuality in and out of the bedroom. It is feeling good about ourselves, feeling *confirmed* as women."[3]

This article indicates that both men and women *want* romance, some more actively than others and certainly in different ways. Women want the unexpected, the intensity of desire, the romantic setting—a walk on a moonlit beach, a candlelight dinner in a quaint chalet, a blanket spread under a grove of trees. But even those things wouldn't be romantic if the talk is business, problems, the kids. No, the conversation has to be about the two of them, about love, about wonderful memories, about desire.

Generally, men's ideas of "romance" and women's ideas are poles apart. When Carole asked me what came to my mind as romantic, I named several *places,* like having hot chocolate in our room overlooking Hong Kong Harbor. Her first thoughts were of *moods*.

Dr. Ed Wheat describes five kinds of love and how each can be *worked on*.[4] One kind of love is "eros," which is romantic love. The other kinds are sexual love, friendship love, security love, and giving or agape love. When there is betrayal or unfaithfulness, trust is destroyed and the security kind of love vanishes. This will, of course, affect romantic love. When struggles come in sexual love, romantic love is also affected. However, even when sexual love and secure love are strong, romantic love can be in a pitiful state.

Each kind of love must be worked on. There is *no letting up*! If a woman says that she loves gardening, but she never does any planting, watering, and weeding, then her talk about love is meaningless.

Many wives and husbands need to begin to water their garden—to work at romance, affection, and intimacy.

For Carole, a great part of keeping the romance in our marriage comes from touching. Cuddling. Eye contact when we hear something funny. An unexpected hug. After one man hugged his wife, the dots on her dress burst into bloom! (Actually, it happened in a cartoon.)

Yes, husbands, touch is *that* important!

But another way to develop the climate of intimacy in our relationships is by frequent glances at our spouses. This is one way to tell if an engaged couple are really in love with one another. Every joke, profound remark, or inane statement is a cause to glance at the other and share a look. Sadly, most couples begin to lose this eye contact after they have been married a few months. If you have grown less frequent in the deep, long, intimate looks or the quick, let's-share-this look, talk about it and begin to glance at each other often when in group discussion (or even watching television). If the other doesn't glance back, give a nudge (if you're close enough) and soon you may again enjoy the warm feeling of sharing these intimate moments.

A great many women long for more affection from their husbands. To them, physical touching is a concrete way of showing *appreciation*. And everyone needs appreciation. David Goodman states it strongly:

There is a psychological law that says: Appreciate and you prosper; belittle and you lose. Unless we learn to apply this law, as psychological as it is spiritual, we are doomed to an existence of mediocrity, frustration, and defeat.

Appreciation is no simple theme, no vague or generalized

theme. Appreciation is a very real force. It is governed by a principle almost as direct as a law of physics: We draw to ourselves the good of everything we appreciate.[5]

"Reserved people need to work on being more demonstrative not just for the sake of *others*, but for *their own sake*, for their own balance, maturity, and development," says family counselor Dr. Gary Oliver. "Just as God *demonstrated* His love for us, part of the process of sanctification involves us learning effective ways to demonstrate our love for one another."[6]

How do reserved people learn to be more expressive and affectionate? Well, logical people take logical steps, right? They get rid of single chairs in front of the television (except for guests, of course). They wouldn't hear of having twin beds or bucket seats in their automobiles. They practice saying hello, good-morning or good-night with at least a hug if not a kiss.

I read of one mother who got into the habit of asking her children each day if their "loving cup" was full. If they said no, she'd hold them in her arms for a time until they were "filled up." Not a bad idea for married people, either.

I realize that I've written much more about the need for the undemonstrative person to work to meet the needs of the affectionate member, but in this case the responsibility does lie with the reserved one for two reasons: (1) the demonstrative nature can't be stifled without serious negative consequences, and (2) intimacy in a marriage grows deeper with demonstrations of affection and love.

Now some of you reserved people are shaking your heads and saying, "How do I do that? And what about my partner accepting the fact that I *am* undemonstrative by nature?"

Leighton Ford said, "God loves and accepts us just the way we are, but He loves us too much to leave us that way!"

So once again, change is demanded. And we can describe the key ingredients as *communication, compromise,* and *reform.*

Communication

Communication about *what is wanted* is the first step. Not in generalities, but in specifics. For Carole that takes a lot of thought, because she just has a *feeling* of what she wants without much thought about what will give her that feeling. Being factual, I need her to tell me specifics.

Take some time to explore with each other questions such as: How important to you is the celebration of special occasions such as birthdays, anniversaries, Valentine's Day? What is your idea of "celebration"? What to you is "romantic"? What would you like for me to do specifically to show affection and care? (Really get down to particulars here, such as: I want you to greet me with a kiss when I come home; I'd like you to hold my hand in public; I'd like you to sit on the couch with me when we watch television.) In these specified items, which is most important to you? Least important?

As you talk to each other about these issues, talk also with God about them. Remember, God is a *creative* God and will give you new, creative thoughts if you ask Him. He is *full* of ideas! And He is just waiting to reveal them to you.

Then, too, talk to older people who evidence love in their marriages. Ask them how they show their partner special love, and write down their answers. Read books.

Compromise

A naturally reserved person is never going to be able to meet all the physical needs that a demonstrative person has to be touched and held, so compromise is necessary. Children and friends help fill the "loving cup" of the affectionate-natured. And so do intimate times spent with God—a God who loves without reserve. True, He doesn't have "skin on," but to feel His arms of love wrapped around us in our spirits is often to have our loving cup filled to overflowing.

Change

We'll keep saying it! The name of the game is change. Perhaps only millimeters at a time—but we can and should be changing. If the affectionate person is changing by learning to have some of those needs met by God and by others; if the reserved person is adding one way of demonstrating affection every few months; then both are growing in understanding and expanding in intimacy.

But whatever steps need taking *must* be taken!

I hope I hear the logical person saying, "That's true."

I know the intuitive one is declaring, "You bet!"

Is the reserved one saying, "I'll try"?

Maybe not. But I'm sure of one thing. The toucher will say, "Hurray! Let's go for it!"

NOTES:

1. Ed Wheat, *Love Life for Every Married Couple* (Grand Rapids: Zondervan Publishing House, 1980), page 183.
2. Lynn Johnston, "For Better or For Worse," *Partnership* (January-February 1988), page 54.
3. Claire Safran, "Must Marriage Kill Romance?" *Redbook* (February 1974), pages 81-84.
4. Wheat, page 57.
5. David Goodman, *A Parent's Guide to the Emotional Development of His Children*, out of print.
6. From seminar notes by Dr. Gary Oliver.

10

What's Your Love Language?
GIVING AND RECEIVING LOVE

CAROLE

When I opened the door, there stood a small boy, dark hair growing every which way, looking at me with big brown eyes. Then he spoke, but whatever he said went right by me.

I smiled and stepped back, motioning him to come inside, and called upstairs to my grandson, "Eric! There's someone at the door for you."

Then I thought, "I sure hope he's here for Eric, and not *selling* something."

For you see, I didn't understand a word the little fellow had said. Jack and I were visiting our kids who live in Mexico, and I don't speak Spanish.

Sometimes I desperately *wish* I spoke Spanish. And I do *desire* to speak Spanish. But I have not paid the price in time or diligence to learn how.

We have no such choice when it comes to learning our partner's language of love, if we want to have a deep and intimate love relationship within our marriage.

A recent article explains the importance of this decision: "People fall in love; but they do not fall into marriage. Marriage involves the will as well as the emotions. Marriages are made. They are made initially by mutual consent and commitment. They still have to be made through the sharing of life and love."[1]

One of the ways to "make a marriage" is by determining to understand your partner's principal language of love so that you can begin to build all the secondary ways to communicate love as well. One man said he felt the first task after the wedding vows was to learn his wife's language—how she primarily expressed love. When he understood this language, then he could begin to accept it, appreciate it, develop it, and learn to express it back.

Dr. Gary Chapman suggests there are five basic love languages: touch, talking (or communication), serving, giving gifts, and encouraging words.[2]

My guess is that if a person were watched closely for as little as twenty-four hours, that person's love language would be discovered. Who do you know who gives you a hug when greeting you, who touches you on the arm to make a point, who "pats" you to express sympathy? That one's main love language is probably touching.

And do you have a friend who wants deep, intimate sharing, who will spend quality time over a cup of coffee even in the midst of a hectic schedule? The love language is talking—communicating.

Perhaps you know a person who finds great delight in serving and doing things for others. You will find that one insisting on cleaning up after a dinner party, mowing a neighbor's lawn, and offering to buy groceries for a shut-in.

Then there is the person who is constantly bringing little gifts; whose mind is always in gear to observe what others need; whose favorite pastime is browsing the garage sales or flea markets to pick up things, not for herself or himself but for others. That person is speaking love by gift-giving.

And who doesn't appreciate an encourager? But have you thought of that as being a leading language of love? The person who thinks to say, "That color is perfect for you," or "I realize that your work is mainly behind the scenes, but I wanted to tell you how much I appreciate it," speaks the language of love in encouragement.

Take a husband whose dominant language is serving, and it takes the form of working many hours each week—often overtime—to support his family. His wife's chief language is talking intimately—communicating—but her husband doesn't have time to do that and doesn't suspect that he needs to. She doesn't comprehend his way of showing love and nags him about working so much. He doesn't fathom her love language either and wonders why she nags him about the time he spends working. Because each fails to understand the other's language, neither feels loved or appreciated.

But when they are *understood*, each can work to esteem the other's language. The wife can be extravagant in her praise of her husband working so hard and doing other things to take care of her and the children. In turn, he must begin to understand her desperate need for intimacy and depth in communicating and plan to spend quality time listening to her "language."

To Mr. Chapman's five languages, we would add some others. You may have even more to include.

As Jack and I discussed the languages of love, we realized that one primary way Jack hears my love is by my being one hundred percent *with him*. Whenever he feels that I am not quite agreeing with what he's doing or the decision that he thought we'd agreed on, he doesn't feel truly loved. Of course we discuss everything, and of course there are times when we don't agree! But when all the discussions are over, he needs to feel I am really *with him* in my heart. And when he asks, a bit plaintively, "Honey, are you really with me on this?" I know I haven't communicated my loyalty—and therefore, to him, my love.

On the other hand, one primary way I hear Jack's love is by his *acceptance* of me. You see, I'm kind of a nut, and I know it. I have an active imagination and sometimes ideas pop into my mind that are, well, let's say *far out*. But to my remembrance, never once in all our married life has Jack said, "Honey, that's got to be the nuttiest idea you ever came up with!" (He may have *thought* it, but he's never *said* it!) I feel his acceptance, which says to me, "I love you" (nutty ideas and all).

When we have learned our partner's language of love, then we can begin to build the secondary languages into our relationship—and have lots of creative, wonderful times doing it. But if we are missing the primary language, our partner may not feel loved in any other way and our efforts will go unnoticed.

We've heard remarks such as:

"My husband is always bringing me flowers or candy. It's like he was trying to buy me off for not spending time with our family."

"I work hard all day and then my wife criticizes me for not being romantic!"

"Why doesn't he *hold me* more when he doesn't want sex? Doesn't he realize I need more nonsexual physical touching?"

"She's always after me to tell her I love her. It's hard for me to be as verbal as she is, but I do try to keep up with all the things in the house that need attention."

Obviously, there may be much more going on in these situations than understanding the other's language. But that might be the first—and simplest—thing to check out. It may just solve the problem.

It's been said, "Neglect the whole world rather than each other." Neglecting the concerted study of our love languages can be harmful to a relationship.

I wonder how many of us know our *own* language of love? I don't think Jack and I were even aware of how many different languages there were until we analyzed them, and even then some time passed before we realized what ours were.

Besides my primary language of acceptance, I probably speak and hear love in three other dialects! High on my list is a great need for deep, intimate sharing, or in Dr. Chapman's list, "talking."

We should note here that our language reveals itself not only with a marriage partner, but also in the type of sharing we want with others. One wife said, "I like intimate groups where we can share deeply." And her husband countered, "I like *large* groups where we *don't* have to share too deeply."[3]

Two of my other languages that would be way up there are not so significant on Jack's list. I speak love through words—the ever important "I love you," and terms of affection as well as compliments—and through touch and tenderness. I like to hear it that way, too.

Jack, on the other hand, is what could be called a *caregiver*. One of the ways Jack shows love is by doing things that protect and watch out for me. He tries to think ahead and anticipate what I am going to need.

Probably another strong way Jack hears and gives love is by companionship. He likes us to do things together—to be together (and I do too)—from reading and watching television to traveling and playing golf.

Several years ago Jack did everything but stand on his head to encourage me to learn to play golf. (He would have done *that* if he'd thought it would have helped.) I finally got the message. He didn't care if I was terrible at golf, which I am. He wanted my companionship.

A number of wives ought to check this one out. Some husbands don't seem to care whether their wife shares in their favorite hobby or sport. But others, if companionship is a strong love language, need a wife who will make that extra effort to join them in recreation.

Because Jack and I have different languages, it is easy for me to fall into two erroneous responses. I can think Jack doesn't love me if he's not speaking my language at the moment, and I can withdraw into a shell because I think he should *know* what I need without my telling him.

"He should *know* what I need" is a statement we hear often. I read of one woman who went for counseling because she felt her husband was being unsupportive in a very painful crisis for her—her mother's illness. She was supposed to fly out to be with her mother, and she was afraid that her mother might die. She asked her husband whether he was coming with her. "Do you want me to?" he said. His wife flew into a rage.

When the counselor asked her if she had said, "Yes, I want you to come," she shook her head in distress. "If I have to ask him, it's not worth it. I want him to come because *he* wants to!"

The counselor asked, "Have you told him how frightened you feel?"

"No!" she said with indignation. "*He should know.*"

She was assuming that her husband didn't care about her because he didn't behave the way *she* would. But the deeper problem, according to this psychologist, was not that her husband was insensitive to her needs, but that she was hypersensitive to his behavior. The whole validity of her wishes and feelings hung on the thread of his response. It wasn't enough that *she* wanted him to come with her; *he* had to want to, or it didn't count. According to the counselor, the real reason she thought her husband "should know" what she was feeling was because she was trying to avoid the painful necessity of expressing her own desires and needs.

Dr. Seymands says that when we become adults, we have the responsibility for communicating our own feelings—but men aren't women, and they often express their caring in a different language. They can be taught, but only slowly and patiently.[4]

At sometime or other, most of us women have been guilty of thinking, "He should know how I feel." And to this day Jack will say occasionally, "Honey, I can't read your mind," which makes me aware of the fact that I was expecting him to do just that. Even after forty years of living with this man, I must remember that assuming he will always know how I feel is not a valid expectation. I must swallow my pride and tell him honestly what it is I'm feeling and *needing* in order for him to understand me. That's what "making a marriage" is all about.

So how do *you* say "I love you"? How does your spouse say it? If you aren't sure, study your spouse this week with intensity and see if you can't discover it.

On your next date, ask each other about the primary way each of you feels love, expresses love. Then ask for opinions of how each of you perceives that the other expresses it and hears it.

I'll guarantee you an interesting conversation.

And a valuable one.

NOTES:
1. Joyce Huggett, "A Promise to Love," *Decision* (July-August 1982).
2. The idea is taken from a cassette tape of Gary Chapman, Focus on the Family Ministries.
3. Chuck and Barb Snyder, *Incompatibility: Grounds for a Great Marriage* (Sisters, OR: Questar Publishers, 1988), page 30.
4. Annie Gottlieb, "He Should Know How I Feel," *McCall's* (August 1984), page 12.

11

Is It Time for a Thaw?
HOW TO MELT THE ICY DIFFERENCES

JACK

Some ideas of marriage are like the attitude of the first-grader who gave this sage advice to his younger brother entering kindergarten: "Whatever you do, don't let them teach you how to spell 'cat.'"

"Why not? Why shouldn't I learn to spell 'cat'?" his brother asked.

"Because," the older one replied, "all the words after that just get harder!"

There are some people in this world who adamantly refuse to change or learn what God would teach them in marriage because . . . it might get harder. In fact, it probably *will* get harder.

I won't try to fool you. Completing and balancing the way we relate to life and to each other is difficult. But if we refuse to learn the lessons, we are missing out on one of God's great purposes for marriage.

We didn't say it first, but we would not hesitate in attesting to the validity of the statement that sums up the marriages of a number of successful "odd" couples: "We fill in each other's missing pieces."

Dr. David Hubbard, president of Fuller Theological Seminary, said, "Marriage does not demand perfection, but it must be given priority. It is an institution for sinners. No one else need apply. But it finds its fullest glory when sinners see it as God's way of leading us to His ultimate curriculum of love and righteousness."[1]

Marriage is a school we attend every day—a school in which God wants the end result to be righteousness, to be *Christlikeness.* To accomplish that purpose, certain regulations are in order—principles from God that must be obeyed.

Now, obeying God is never easy. But the good news is, we don't have to do it alone. He gave us His Holy Spirit to live within us so that we are able to respond *supernaturally* rather than in our own natural, selfish, stubborn way.

The story is told of a small boy flying a kite so high above the clouds it couldn't be seen.

A passerby asked, "Why are you holding onto that string?"

"Because," the boy replied, "there's a kite on the other end."

"How do you know? I don't see it," the man teased.

"I know because I can feel the tug," the boy answered.

If we are open to God, we feel the tug of His Holy Spirit definitely and consistently in our lives. He constantly nudges us to be kind, forgiving, and sensitive, and to be helpers—and completers—of one another.

But God doesn't leave us in the dark regarding the rules He wants us to obey. He has spelled them out for us in Scripture.

One all-encompassing and critical command that I think all husbands and wives should practice diligently every day of their lives together is Ephesians 4:32—"Be kind to one another, be understanding. Be as ready to forgive others as God, for Christ's sake, has forgiven you" (PH).

If we could consistently practice just that *one* verse, we would have some of the happiest marriages going.

Be kind. How often we are the least kind to those we love the most.

Be understanding. Many Bible versions translate this word "compassionate" or "tenderhearted," which means sympathizing deeply, sorrowing for the troubles of another, accompanied by an urge to help.

I would estimate that ninety percent of conflicts come because two people approach life in contrasting ways. When we obey the command to *understand,* we solve a great percentage of marital disputes. In order to understand, we have to *listen. Really listen.*

How well do *you* listen? Have you ever tried rephrasing what your spouse is saying? If you have, you'll know that sometimes a person has to try two or three times before the partner says, "Yes, *now* you understand."

But the question comes often, "I've listened and I do understand. But what if it *isn't* just different? What if it really is *wrong?*"

Therein lies the rub.

All right, so the other person is *wrong*. Your spouse has done something incredibly selfish and hurtful that God declares in the Bible to be *sin*. You know it. Your partner knows it. The wound goes deep.

When we are hurt, we build walls around our emotions so if it happens again we won't ache so much. But when the damage continues, the walls keep rising until they are so high and so thick, we begin to live as strangers.

What can we do? No matter how difficult it may be, the Bible says we are to *be forgiving.* The third part of Ephesians 4:32 reads, "Be as ready to forgive others as God, for Christ's sake, has forgiven you."

How much has God forgiven you for Christ's sake? Totally, completely. Forgiveness is the answer to pulling down those walls of separation—or preventing them from rising in the first place.

"Forgiveness." It's a simple word to say, isn't it? But the task is complex, penetrating, difficult—and yes, even impossible to do. Impossible for *us* anyway. But not for God. And everyday forgiveness of little things is as necessary as forgiveness of the major sins, mistakes, and errors of our mates. I'll give you a hint: It is easier to forgive *before* that first brick has been mortared in than after the wall is in place.

David Augsburger eloquently defines forgiveness:

> Stated in marriage relationships, forgiveness takes place when love accepts—deliberately—the hurts and abrasions of life and drops all charges against the other person. Forgiveness is accepting the other when both of you know he or she has done something unacceptable.
>
> Forgiveness is smiling silent love to your partner when the justifications for keeping an insult or injury alive are on the tip of your tongue, yet you swallow them. Not because you have to, to keep peace, but because you want to, to make peace.
>
> Forgiveness is not acceptance given "on condition" that the other becomes acceptable. Forgiveness is given freely. Out

of a deep awareness that the forgiver also has need of constant forgiveness, daily.

Forgiveness exercises God's strength to love and receive the other person without any assurance of complete restitution and making of amends.

Forgiveness is a relationship between equals who recognize their deep need of each other, share and share alike. Each needs the other's forgiveness. Each needs the other's acceptance. Each needs the other.

And so, before God, each drops all charges, refuses all self-justification and forgives. And forgives. Seventy times seven.[2]

Refusal to forgive automatically causes bitterness. Someone has said that bitterness harms the vessel it's stored in much more than the one it is poured out upon. And friends, stored-up bitterness eats through like acid.

I wonder how many of us realize that our bitterness against the offender is as great a sin in God's eyes as the original offense. The Bible says, "See to it that no one misses the grace of God and that no bitter root grows up to cause trouble and defile many" (Hebrews 12:15). Bitterness will first of all hurt *you*, then your spouse, then many others. It's like a pebble dropped in water causing ever-widening ripples.

Jim Hilt, staff counselor of Chapel of the Air, recommends four basic steps for healing bitterness.

First, *confess it*. Do not justify or explain it away.

Second, *ask God for the power to accept the source of the bitterness*. Accept the wounds and hurt through God's power. *Acceptance is not the same as approval*, nor should God be thanked for the offense. Thank God that He can work through evil to bring about good in our lives. Christ *accepted* His sufferings, which allowed Him to endure.

Third, *ask God for the power to forgive the offender*. On our own resources, we cannot forgive. Even if the offender hasn't apologized, forgive anyway. Forgiveness releases a lot of steam inside. Forgive by name.

Fourth, *ask God to liberate you from your prison walls*, to heal all bitterness from past and present. Otherwise you will be bound up to that bitterness.

I'm dwelling on the need for forgiveness here because the lack of it is often the major hurdle to building positive qualities in our marriages or even seeing our differences in a constructive light. If we've allowed walls to rise between us, then *everything* is going to seem wrong. Those walls must be torn down before we can begin to see ways to complete each other in how we think and relate.

One verse, three commands: *Be kind. Be understanding. Be forgiving.* Each command is imperative for a loving and intimate marriage.

The warmth of living out these God-given instructions will infiltrate the very pores of the introvert and the extrovert, the affectionate and the reserved. It will be felt even when your languages of love have no phrases in common.

Here are a few suggestions for melting the icy differences:

Set objectives. Write down practical steps you can take to grow in relating. Plan to attend a marriage seminar; do a Bible study on the person of Christ (to see the perfect balance in a life, for instance); memorize together some verses on understanding; pray together daily concerning understanding. Have someone close to you check up on your progress.

Start now and do it! A godly friend of ours was asked by a young woman, "My mother and I fight all the time and clash every single day. What can I do?" His advice to her was, "Stop it!"

Remember, we *can* if we *will*. Our wills are involved in the process of putting into action what God wants us to change.

Finally, *celebrate* your differences.

Toward the end of her life and a second marriage, Catherine Marshall wrote, "Husbands and wives are basically incompatible. . . . That's why the home is His classroom for moulding and shaping us into mature people."[3]

Let's celebrate God's molding.

Carl Rogers uses this analogy: "When I walk on the beach to watch the sunset I do not call out, 'A little more orange over to the right, please,' or, 'Would you mind giving us less purple in the back?' No, I enjoy the always-different sunsets as they are. We do well to do the same with people we love."[4]

Let's celebrate God's unique designs.

Marriage is a climb—sometimes a steep one. But, holding on to the hand of God, the sights are wonderful up there.

They are, that is, if we learn how to stay on the heights with God—who is the blessed Controller of all things.

NOTES:

1. David Hubbard, quoted in *Marriage Takes More Than Love* (Colorado Springs, CO: NavPress, 1978), pages 139-140.

2. David Augsburger, *Cherishable: Love and Marriage* (Scottsdale, PA: Herald Press, 1971), page 146.

3. William J. Peterson, *Catherine Marshall Had a Husband* (Wheaton, IL: Tyndale House Publishers, 1986), quoted in *The Christian Reader*, page 46.

4. Alan Loy McGinnis, *The Romance Factor* (New York: Harper and Row, 1982), quoted in "How to Weather Marital Storms," *Readers Digest*.

PART III

THE WAY WE TALK

12

Cat and Mouse, Anyone?

REVEALER VS. CONCEALER

JACK

There was no hope in his eyes as he faced me.

"She walked out on me," he said. "Just called me at work one day and said, 'I've had it. I'm leaving.'" He tried to control the tremor around his mouth.

"I realize now that much of it was my fault. I guess she tried to tell me. . . ."

As I listened, I realized the truth of what he'd said. She *had* tried to tell him. When their son was born, she hadn't wanted to go back to work immediately, but he pressured her, telling her that they needed her income. She nagged some and later grew severely depressed, but he didn't think her depression had anything to do with him or with being away from their son.

Actually, that wife had pushed every button she had available to make him listen to her pain and anger. But he was oblivious to her inner cries. He worked two jobs so he wasn't home much—but more importantly, <u>even when he was home, he failed her emotionally.</u>

Somewhere in time, she decided that the pain of divorce was more bearable than the hurt of being in the same house when they were emotionally at opposite ends of the earth.

So . . . she walked out. What she did wasn't right, but I can understand it. It was probably a last desperate attempt to get her husband's attention. She got it, all right, but it came too late.

I wonder how many broken relationships are due to a similar scenario. I wonder how many men are in the process this very moment of distancing their wives by failing to understand their needs—the need to be listened to, to have feelings and emotions validated by their husband's concentrated attention and understanding.

Not that men don't need emotional support and intimacy—they do, of course. I know some men who have as great a need for relating on an emotional, feeling, subjective level as *any* woman. They are often the counselors, those others turn to when in trouble, the pastor-shepherds. But as Carole and I have listened to couples, we find that in the average marriage, it's generally a matter of *degree*. And the women's need usually seems greater. It is she who most often longs for soul-to-soul communication and who feels like she never quite has that desire met by her spouse.

This incident appeared in a recent article:

Judy, an artist, was worried about preparations for an exhibition, and started to tell Cliff, her husband. She wanted his support and sympathy.

Instead, Cliff fired off instructions: "One, get all the artists together. Two, call your accountant—the expenses may be deductible. Three, check with the bank to see how much money you have. Four, contact the P.R. people."

Judy felt rejected, and thought to herself: "Cliff doesn't care how I feel. He just wants to get me off his back."

Cliff believed he *was* being supportive—he had given her his best advice. But Judy was seeking emotional rapport, not problem solving.[1]

Carole and I can relate to that! I have had to work on intimacy in communication all of our married life. It probably has to do with me being that logical, factual, objective kind of guy. I have to admit that by nature, I am a concealer of my feelings. In fact, if one side of a scale represented the ability to express feelings and the other side represented the need to conceal those feelings, Carole and I would probably balance the scales pretty well.

According to most marriage counselors, concealment is more often a trait in men, and it stems from various factors such as background, cultural expectations, perceptions of manliness, and personality. This tendency to conceal has drastic implications. James Collier says that most men think it unmanly even to admit that they *have* a problem—much less request aid:

> Men in America feel that they ought to be able to deal with anything that comes along, and it's an admission of failure if they're having trouble. Some men would rather fail at their marriage or with their children than admit that something is wrong and seek a solution.
> . . . Says marriage specialist Goldstein, "Men aren't supposed to have sensitive, warm feelings or feelings of tenderness for the people around them—much less express them." It is like the story of the old Vermont farmer 40 years married, who said, "I love Sarah Jane so much that sometimes it's all I can do to keep from telling her."[2]

Communication patterns. Spell them d-i-f-f-e-r-e-n-t.

■ Different in the number of and reasons for questions. A revealer is often full of questions and sees them as a way to maintain a conversation, thinking "If I don't ask, the other person won't know that I care." Questions represent intimacy and caring.

But not to a concealer! Now questions can represent meddling. The concealer may be thinking, "Oh, no, you don't! You can't pry that information out of me. If I want to tell you something, I'll tell you—without all your questions."

■ Different, too, in the nature of responses to communication.

A revealer may use encouraging sounds such as "uh-huh" and "hmmm" to encourage the other person—and then feel ignored because the concealer utters so few of these acknowledging sounds. When I listen silently, Carole sometimes asks, "Honey, are you *there*?"

■ Different in the use of what some call "oneness" words such as *you* and *we*. A revealer may use many more of such words, as well as conversational bridges such as "Please go on . . . would you give me another example? . . ."

Can you identify yourself? As I've said, I tend to be the concealer, and—being logical as well—I have to say that often, logical men have

logical reasons for concealment! I read of a group of men who were
asked their reasons for not talking. Several of them gave fairly logical
reasons, such as simply not being in a talkative mood, or being tired
and not wanting to expend energy talking, even wanting to protect the
wife when she was tired and agitated and her emotional tank was near
"empty."

But others in the group answered in ways that indicated their concealment should not be accepted at face value. Listen to these reasons
some men gave:

(1) Silence helps me avoid differences of opinion. I grew up in a
family that rarely expressed strong feelings. So talking is tough,
especially when I know what I have to say isn't what my wife
wants to hear.

(2) Silence protects me. Sometimes I don't want to talk to
my wife about certain things because I'm afraid she will use
them against me.

(3) Silence maintains a balance of attachment and freedom
that feels comfortable in our relationship. Sometimes I need closeness, but other times I need distance. I'm most content with our
marriage when there is a natural ebb and flow in our interaction.

(4) Silence precludes heated explosions. If I don't shoot off
words, I'm less likely to catch crossfire or have to pick up debris
when the battle ceases.

(5) When something is bothering me, I don't talk because
my wife tends to overreact and make matters worse. The last
thing I want is someone bouncing off the walls in anger or else
sniveling about it.[3]

Did you notice a similarity in these five reasons for silence? It
would appear that most of these reasons are based on *self* protection or
comfort, not on the intimacy of the marriage or the needs of the wife.

Now of course there are times when silence is good. But to constantly conceal our feelings is bound to stifle the intimacy and closeness
that our marriages demand (and most wives need) in order for us to
become truly one.

One counselor puts it this way: Wives think, "The marriage is
working as long as we can talk about it." Husbands think, "The rela-

tionship is not working if we have to keep talking about it."[4]

So we're different. So one of us doesn't talk much about feelings, and the other shares freely. Can anything be done?

Family counselor Norm Wright says,

> A woman does not have to resign herself to living with an unexpressive male. Becoming fatalistic is not the answer, and I'm not talking about divorcing him either. Don't listen if someone tells you, "Don't be so concerned about men not expressing their feelings. That's just the way they are!" Men may tend to be that way, but they can change. Challenges or reproaches do not work. Carefully worded invitations can work. Men do respond initially to questions which elicit factual responses. It's easier for a man to tell his wife what he does at work than how he feels about it. He can tell her how he did at events or school when he was growing up easier than how he feels about what he did. But starting with the facts is an introduction to the feelings.[5]

But the revealer must be cautioned: Mr. Wright also says that a man may finally open up to a woman only to find that what he reveals is discounted, shared with others, disbelieved, ridiculed, rejected, and even laughed at. Remember: safety, acceptance, and support are essential if a man is going to let down the bridge from his castle. He wants what he shares to be used *for* his welfare, not against him. Trust is a major issue.[6]

Let's get practical. What does intimate, deep sharing actually look like?

Intimate, according to *Webster,* means pertaining to the inmost character of a thing; most private or personal. One of the meanings of "deep" is "great in degree, intense." So in order to have intimate, deep, sharing, first I have to know what's going on in my innermost heart (and God will help me get in touch with that if I ask Him), and then I must be willing to open up about it.

Scary? You bet. Difficult? Absolutely. I may strain and struggle; stop, start, and stop again. I may fall back one step for every two forward strides I take. I may take months or even years. But with God's help and my determination, I *can* do it.

I can share my experiences of yesterday and today—my successes, my failures, my ideas, my hopes and dreams. I can tell my spouse when I'm afraid (even afraid to confide!), when I'm discouraged, when I feel inadequate, intimidated, or angry. I can share my elation, my joy, my delights. I can tell her of the moments today when I wanted to cry, the absurdities I wanted to scream at, the scenes that made me chuckle. And I can ask my partner to share with me some of the same feelings she has experienced. When each of us commits to this, true oneness of soul and spirit will begin.

The Bible defines marriage as two becoming one. But how is this possible with conversation that is only mouth to ear—surface things, cliché communication?

We need so much more than that. We need more than his mind to her mind, which is only facts and ideas, or her heart to his heart, which is only feelings.

What we really need for intimacy and oneness in marriage is one soul . . . *intertwining* with another soul.

That's intimacy.

And that is oneness.

NOTES:

1. Aaron T. Beck, "Why Husbands Won't Talk," *Readers Digest* (December 1988), page 9.
2. James Lincoln Collier, "Why Men Won't Seek Help," *Readers Digest* (September 1975), page 140.
3. Pam Walker Vredevelt, "Husbands Who Speak Through Silence," *Partnership* (July-August 1987), page 27.
4. Collier, page 140.
5. H. Norman Wright, *Understanding the Man in Your Life* (Waco, TX: Word Books, 1987), page 101.
6. Wright, page 100.

13

Once Again...
With Feeling
SPEAKING FACTS VS. FEELINGS

CAROLE

The day was dreary and cold. Rain splattered against the windowpane. I glanced outside and said to Jack, "It's raining outside."

Now Jack is not blind, nor is he deaf. He was well aware of the weather outside.

So why was I stating the obvious? Making conversation? Not really. Believe it or not, I was stating a *feeling*. I was really saying, "That rain makes me feel depressed."

I often use speech to convey feelings. On that day, I could have been saying any number of things, such as "the rain makes me feel energetic and I'm going to plow into the housecleaning this morning," or "the rain is making me feel reflective and I'd like to sit by the fire and go through old school annuals." But chances are, in a statement like that, I am expressing a feeling.

Not Jack! He uses speech most often to express *fact*. If he says, "It's raining outside," he means the clouds have opened and little drops of moisture are falling to the ground.

This difference in the way we use speech is a critical one in our relationships—one that must be learned and relearned, accepted, understood, and then remembered . . . and remembered . . . and remembered.

I read about a minister who had to go to a nearby city to conduct a funeral. He asked his wife to go along with him. "If you want me to," she said.

"Well," the man said, after a moment of silence, "I'll go alone."

The author pointed out that each had been needlessly disappointed. The husband wanted his wife with him and hoped she would offer to accompany him. She wanted to go but, not sure he really meant the invitation, tossed the decision to him. He assumed she was turning him down; she assumed he didn't need her support. And so a couple who wanted to express their mutual love and need wound up feeling each had been rejected by the other.[1]

Can you interpret this little exchange? The minister was a factual speaker. He would not have asked his wife to go with him for any reason other than because he wanted her to go. His wife, not so factual in her approach to life, was looking for internal reassurance that he wanted her company.

All you have to do is listen to the conversations around you in public places to find out who are the fact speakers and who are the feeling speakers.

As I was walking down an airport corridor recently, I overheard two men talking behind me. The first man said, "I'm not exactly looking forward to this meeting."

The second asked enthusiastically, "Aren't you *excited* about the possibilities we're examining?"

The first man responded in a flat tone of voice, "I don't know."

I could *feel* the pinprick in the balloon of the second man's enthusiasm. I imagined the look on his face. Yet the first man was simply being honest and factual. One was speaking facts as he saw them, the other speaking feelings as he felt them.

Picture a couple gazing at some paintings in an art gallery. A companion asks, "Do you like this first one?"

One says, "Yes."

The other says, "Oh, wow, it's gorgeous!"

"And how about this second one?"

The first says, "No."

The other says, "Yuk! It's *awful*!"

"Well, how about this third abstract?"

One says, "I don't know."

The other says, "Hmmm, well, it's interesting, but I'll have to have some time to see how I feel about it."

Those of us who use speech to convey *feelings* have a hard time saying things like, "I don't know." "Yes." "No." "Not very." Any simple factual statement is difficult because if it doesn't convey feeling, it isn't a fact to us. How we *feel* is the fact. (Did you factual people get that? Probably not!)

I can't tell you how difficult it is for me sometimes either to tell or listen to just the plain, unadulterated *facts* about something. To me, they're just not very interesting! I'm working on it—but let me tell you, it's hard!

In a humorous article, Jean Kerr suggests couples ought to have a readiness test for marriage, much like a driver's test. Some of her suggested questions are funny, but in a comical way, profound—and they show how feelings can sometimes masquerade as thinly-disguised "facts." She asks men to select the proper answer when their wife makes the following observations:

"I suppose you wish I were as good a cook as Emmy."

(a) Or even half as good.

(b) I'm sure you could cook as well as Emmy does if you were willing to put in the same amount of time.

(c) Oh, I'd get pretty sick of all that rich food day after day. And they say Bill's getting a liver condition.

"Do you love me as much as the day we were married?"

(a) Yeah.

(b) Oh, no, not again.

(c) If you have to ask that question, honey, it must be my fault. I mustn't be showing all the love I really feel.

"You never talk to me."

(a) I don't talk to you because the only topics that interest you are Billy's rotten report card, your rotten dishwasher, and that rotten milkman who keeps tracking up your linoleum.

(b) Of course I talk to you. What am I doing now— pantomime?

(c) And here I was, sitting here and thinking how beautiful you are and how lucky I am and how peaceful it was.[2]

Some of the responses are, of course, cruel. But one in each case is factual—and factual speakers would think those answers were A-OK! But feeling speakers want the "c" answers every time.

My guess is that I have spent more time crying over this difference than any other one. And I still have to remind myself of this one occasionally.

I remember an incident years ago when Jack had been away for a couple of weeks. Lynn and I decided we would fix up the guest room and surprise Jack with a refurbished room. We painted it, put up new curtains, even used our scrupulously saved S & H Green Stamps for new bedspreads. After we had greeted him on his return, we pulled him upstairs, dramatically threw open the door to the guest room, and with great gusto said, "Well, what do you think?"

He looked around carefully, nodded, and said quietly, "I like it."

I looked at Lynn and she looked back at me. Then we burst out laughing. You see, we'd just been studying some differences—including this one—and we quickly realized that Jack was stating a fact, and that was okay. I would have gone on and on about the colors, the work, the curtains, the decor to have convinced someone I liked it.

Some of us have to have it *with feeling*, or we don't believe it.

The apostle Peter uses an interesting little phrase in 1 Peter 3:7—"live with your wives in an *understanding* way."

I wonder how many husbands obey that command. We hear so many men say, "I just don't understand why she gets so emotional about things," or "I can't comprehend why she doesn't believe me when I say I like her dress."

And their wives often women relate, "He isn't on my wavelength at all," or "He doesn't seem to feel anything deeply."

It may not be true of all factual speakers, but Jack *does* feel things deeply. I've seen him kneeling at the foot of Lynn's bed when at age ten she broke off a front tooth trying to do a handstand on the basement floor. She was asleep, and his face showed his anguish and concern for her (he'd lost a tooth in college and wondered how her loss might affect her).

I've seen him so torn up that he couldn't say anything at all in a situation that I was taking a bit more philosophically.

Oh yes, he definitely *feels*. But his verbal expressions of those feelings come out as facts. Calm (most of the time), steady, precise.

No ranting or railing for him. Just the facts.

I heard of an incident concerning a renowned author of books on marriage. Years ago, this man and his wife took the kind of temperament analysis in which each person takes the test twice: the first time for oneself and the second time projecting how one's spouse would answer. The wife rated her husband as having few feelings, but when his test came back, his score in the feeling category went right off the chart. She finally realized that her husband *had* all kinds of deep feelings, but he rarely *expressed* them—and so she began to learn how to ask questions that would help him express those feelings to her.

If Jack and I had taken that test, undoubtedly we would have had similar results. Through the years, however, Jack has learned to verbalize his feelings to me as I ask questions—but he is still a "fact" speaker.

A recent event brought that to mind once again.

This year we attended Jack's fortieth college reunion. It was a time of renewing friendships and sharing intervening years. But it was also a time, for me, of facing my own mortality. I didn't like having to look at name tags in order to recognize people. And I liked it even less that they had to do that with me! I came away from that weekend thinking soberly of the aging process.

I shared my melancholy thoughts with Jack. He listened and then said, "Yes, but you've got to remember the saying on that little plaque Mom has in her kitchen: 'Age is mind over matter. If you don't mind, it doesn't matter.'"

End of discussion. I could tell his mind had already switched to another topic.

I almost screamed, "No! That doesn't *help.* You aren't listening to what I'm *feeling*—my fears and my questions about the future. I need you to understand what's going on *inside* of me right now."

But this time I remained silent. Because Jack *did* understand how I felt. He was just reminding me of a fact—a fact that is true and right. A fact I needed to be reminded of.

Over the years I've learned that deep understanding—that Jack speaks facts and I speak feelings—is critical to our relationship. I couldn't *accept* that until I *understood* it.

Even now, it's not easy. But friends, it's *possible.*

And that's a fact!

NOTES:
1. Gail MacDonald, *The Pastor's Wife and the Church*, out of print.
2. Jean Kerr, "Marriage—Unsafe at Any Speed," *Readers Digest* (May 1970), vol. 96, page 60.

14

Translation, Please?

TIPS FOR OVERCOMING YOUR
LANGUAGE BARRIERS

CAROLE

The tall, upholstered sides of the booth walled out the world as Jack and I settled into the soft seat cushions. I sighed happily in anticipation of dinner and the evening ahead.

Halfway through my "surf and turf," I asked Jack a question that I'd been mulling over for some time.

"Honey, I know that one of the primary ways you hear my love is when you know I'm one hundred percent behind you—when I'm not pulling in another direction. But besides that language of love, what is another way in which you hear love the best?"

Jack was silent for several moments. Then he said thoughtfully, "I know how you hear *my* love."

"That isn't exactly what I asked, but that'll do for a start," I responded. "How do you think I hear your love?"

"I *know* how you hear my love," he said emphatically. "You hear it by intimate heart-to-heart communication—like we are doing now."

I reflected briefly. "You're right, of course. And you? Do you hear love that way?"

"I do *now*," Jack replied.

"Why now?" I persisted.

"After living with you all these years, and having found out the oneness and depth it brings to our relationship, I wouldn't want to live any other way."

"But before," I pressed. "If you hadn't married a revealer—one who hears love through communicating intimately—would you have heard or given love that way?"

"I don't know," he said. "I only know I speak and hear it that way now."

(We had to go back to Jack's logical, sensing personality here, and I accepted it. Jack can't imagine the "what if's" very well—and generally he doesn't try to.)

I touched Jack's hand, leaned toward him and said, "Well, I'm certainly glad you speak and hear that language now, sweetheart."

I've always craved intimacy and depth in sharing. And I'm so grateful that over the years Jack has learned to need it, too. I know it has been commitment, determination, and a deliberate choice on his part to learn.

A wife can help her husband learn to share deeply. But nagging doesn't do it. Withdrawing won't either. Nor will overwhelming him with questions and ideas.

I haven't always assisted in the best way, but over the years I've found some that work:

Be sensitive to your partner's moods. I remember one time when I prepared for a date by collecting a couple of what I thought were terrific, fun, off-the-wall questions—the kind that often do open up communication for us. I was determined not to talk about the problems at the office that had consumed much of our conversation that week.

So when the time came, I brightly asked my questions. Jack looked at me dully and mumbled a response. Another question. Another monotone answer.

Although there had been times when I'd get irritated and withdraw because of such a response, I was trying to understand and learn. So finally I said, "Okay, honey. Obviously you're not in the mood for this kind of conversation. So let's talk about what is really on your mind." For the rest of the evening we went back over the problems that were heaviest on his heart.

We try not to let the "heavies" dominate dates, but we know how important it is to be tuned in to the other's moods.

Asking questions to draw out your partner is part of sensitivity to his or her moods. But don't be insensitive in the way you ask them! Ask good questions, but don't overwhelm your spouse with too many all at once.

Be available to your more quiet partner. Sometimes when I'm in the middle of a writing project, I whisk upstairs to get something, my thoughts deep into what I'm researching. (I deliberately located my study in the basement so I don't have to clean things up when I'm finished for the day. Jack's office is upstairs in our two-story home.) Catching sight of me, Jack will say, "Can you sit down a minute? I've got something to show you." My inclination is to say, "It'll have to wait—I'm right in the middle of a project." But I fight this urge because I know Jack needs to talk when he's in the frame of mind for it. And we've had some great spontaneous talks in his study. I make this deliberate choice to encourage my less-verbal husband to share deeply. If I cut him off at times like those, I think he would be less inclined to share when I'm the one who wants to communicate.

Remember that in encouraging a spouse to open up, a close companion of availability is trust. Jack and I have worked at making each of us feel safe with the other. We have vowed not to put down what we hear or repeat confidential information to others.

Learn your partner's love language. Jack has worked so hard to learn my language of love that it's now a part of him and he would miss it if we didn't have frequent times of soul-sharing.

But I am beginning to believe that the way most husbands define "good communication" is about as similar to the way most wives define it, as a giraffe is to a hippopotamus. They're both animals, but the similarity begins and ends there.

Take a person who is emotional and subjective. Throw in her language of love: intimate, deep, feeling-type conversation.

Then add a spouse who is objective, logical, and factual: his primary love language is caregiving and protection.

Send them out for dinner, and give them three hours to talk. They haven't really talked for some time, so they both start off with empty communication cups. Let's watch what happens.

An hour goes by while they catch up on what has been happening at work, with their schedules, with the kids, with their friends.

His cup is now fifty percent full; hers is at the most five percent.

They spend another hour discussing a problem he's having with a client, considering what they want to do on their next vacation, and evaluating the status of their financial planning.

His cup is now up to eighty-five percent; hers is fifteen percent.

During their third hour they share what they're learning in Bible study and what they'd like to see happen in the small group they're part of. Dinner's over.

His cup is ninety-five percent full—and hers?? Maybe twenty-five percent.

As they leave the restaurant, he thinks, "What a great time of in-depth communication we've had!"

She's thinking—and feeling—"We've only just begun! And now we won't have time to *really* talk!"

He says, "We'll have to do this again next month."

She says, "How about tomorrow?"

For you feeling-sharers, I don't need to spell out what's happened here. But for you fact-oriented people, let me explain.

The wife loved every minute of the three-hour conversation. But she needed more. To fill *her* communication cup, part of that three hours would need to have been spent sharing the joys, sorrows, frustrations, delights, and wonders of everything from the problems at work to the insights of Bible study to the concerns for the children. Added to *that*, she would want to explore her varying responses to each of those joys, sorrows, frustrations, delights, and wonders. To top it off, the final portion would be her husband sharing his feelings about these issues. Then her cup would be overflowing!

Here's a tremendous question for a facts-person to ask of a feeling-person: "On a scale of one to ten with ten being high, how are you feeling at this moment about yourself as a parent . . . in your job . . . as a friend . . . as a child of parents . . . as a spouse . . . in your walk with God?" Then, to put the icing on the cake, share with your spouse how *you* feel about one or two of the above.

If you ask any ten couples to rate their success in communicating, I'll bet that in eight or nine cases the husband will say, "Oh, we're doing great. I'd rate us at least an eight or nine on a scale of ten." And the wife will look embarrassed because in her mind she's rating them a two.

Why? Most women think they haven't really *communicated* unless they've shared on a feeling level. But most men are satisfied with stating and discussing the facts.

So how do you come to terms with this great disparity? Slowly, perhaps. Expect it to take time—maybe even years—because both of you must change.

The subjective, feeling-oriented person must deal with—and in many cases change—*expectations*.

We once asked a counselor of engaged couples what was the difficulty he ran into most frequently. Without a moment's hesitation he replied, "Unrealistic expectations."

Engaged couples aren't alone in this area. One married couple drove four hours to see us about some difficulties they were having. During the drive, the wife let out all her frustrations, feelings, and thoughts to her husband, who patiently listened and responded. As they spoke to us later she said, "Oh, if we could just do this every day, we wouldn't have any problems." Her husband rolled his eyes heavenward, and I smiled as I said, "Your husband would go *crazy* if he had to spend four hours every day talking about feelings." He nodded emphatically.

That wife needed to deal with her unrealistic expectations. Rare is the person who can explore deep feelings for several hours a day. There are more who can do it several hours a week, but for most fact-oriented people, several hours a months is more realistic, and those hours would need to be broken into several segments. (For this reason, I am convinced a feeling-type woman needs a close female friend who is like her to relieve the husband of being the only one with whom she can explore emotions.)

But while many must face up to their own unrealistic expectations, objective people have to become aware of needs not their own, develop a desire to meet those needs, and pray for the willingness both to listen to the feelings of a spouse and also to express their own emotions.

This requires *unselfishness*, for it's difficult to take the time to probe and listen. But intimacy and oneness demand it. Sharing just facts is only scratching the surface. The dissatisfied partner may become unhappy and start pushing destructive buttons in order to get attention.

Both kinds of people need patience. Logical people need patience to listen to things they may not be tuned into. Feeling people need patience for the long process involved as the factual person learns to share emotions.

A further contributing factor to the difficulties in this area is that most of us fall within the categories of amplifier or condenser. An amplifier states something and then goes on to explain it; a condenser shortens everything to the minimum. According to Norm Wright, less-verbal partners often don't want to bring up certain issues because they are afraid a ten-minute topic will take an hour. Verbal partners become so starved for communication that when their partner does open up, they jump in with both feet, which makes the nonverbal one wary of opening up again.[1]

Mr. Wright suggests one way to handle this difference:

> If the verbal person goes to the spouse and says, "Honey, I want to talk to you for ten minutes, and even if I'm in the middle of a sentence after ten minutes, I promise I will stop. Would you try it?"
>
> At first, the spouse might be wary and mistrusting. But if the verbal partner will follow through, the husband or wife will probably go along with it. And after a few of those experiences, one might say, "Hey, I can talk for another ten minutes, let's follow through with this discussion." The quiet one needs to know that if he/she opens up, control of the situation will not be lost but that the other will understand that verbalizing feelings is hard.[2]

One couple we were helping in this area asked us, "Okay; let's say we have two hours each week and we want to spend it working on our marriage. What, specifically, do we do in those two hours?"

We couldn't help it! We laughed! Then we apologized and began to talk about how working at your marriage is a twenty-four-hours-a-day job. You work at it in a hundred different ways continually—by the commitment to talk, to work through conflict, to understand, to forgive. Working to understand the *way* we talk is crucial. Comprehending this crucial area will help us relate more easily to others, both inside and outside our family.

Concealers marry revealers, by God's design.

Fact-speakers wed feeling-speakers, and each brings specific strengths to the relationship.

True, conflicts arise from these differences. But working through conflict brings growth. The deeper the conflict, the more understanding and intimacy we experience afterward.

May God enable us to make it so!

NOTES:

1. Article interview with H. Norman Wright in *Partnership* (Summer 1988), pages 25-28.
2. *Partnership*, pages 25-28.

15

Can We Talk About This Later?

CONFRONTERS, WITHDRAWERS, AND THE WAY WE FIGHT

CAROLE

U-R-P. You've never heard of it, right? (Or did you think I'd just hiccuped?) Vernon Cronen, a professor of communication studies at the University of Massachusetts, coined the term in 1979.[1] The initials stand for Unwanted Repetitive Patterns, which is a fancy way of saying that we tend to get stuck in a rut in the way we fight, mostly because of the way we've been wired together from day one.

There are as many ways to fight as there are personalities. Some simmer; some explode. Some attack head-on, others blind-side. But two opposing styles we are all familiar with are what some call the confronter and the avoider, or the attacker and the retreater. Others label these dual approaches the expressive and the nonexpressive: "Usually the nonexpressive person will want to walk away from conflict, while the expressive wants to talk about it, find out what's wrong, and be friends again . . . nonexpressives do not want to talk about it, and believe that if they don't, it will go away. They feel if they just let it alone, everyone will remain friends."[2]

Whatever you name them, they're easy to identify, and so are their techniques.

The positive aspect of what we'll call the confronter is that conflict issues are brought out into the open, talked about, and ideally, worked through to a conclusion. But confronters want to confront *right now*—anytime, anywhere, and anything—and sometimes their timing is *awful*.

The withdrawer knows that at times silence *is* golden because issues can look monstrous when you're tired, sick, or struggling with other pressing problems. Sometimes a little distance is all you need to see that the Creature From The Lost Lagoon is really just a small, ordinary toad.

Both types, however, often use unfair techniques.

The confronter is frequently an expert at bringing up the past. One man said, "When we quarrel, my wife becomes historical."

"Don't you mean hysterical?" his friend asked.

"No, I mean historical—she brings up everything I ever did."

Confronters are also adept at hauling in secondary issues: "And not only won't you help around the house, you forgot to pick me up from the hairdresser's last week!"

The expressives tend to exaggerate and intimidate. They may yell, scream, and even use an "ultimate" threat such as, "Well, maybe we ought to get a divorce," or "You'd like me to commit suicide, wouldn't you?"

Some may also use humiliation to intimidate with exaggerated statements such as "How can you be so stupid?"

Withdrawers have their own modus operandi. Obviously, the over-all approach is to duck the confrontation in any way possible—being too busy to talk, postponing the discussion, mumbling "Why don't we talk about this another time?" or "Let's not make a big deal out of this."

When forced, they will often sidestep the issue by (1) changing the subject, (2) interrupting and thus not allowing the other to finish the statement, (3) crying, or (4) waving the white flag of surrender before the discussion is over. Withdrawers may also simply refuse to talk about it, ignore it, sulk, pout, or give the cold shoulder for days on end.

Both confronters and withdrawers use the tactic of sarcasm and ridicule. Both may be quick to jump to a conclusion, try to read the other's mind, grab the old standbys "always" and "never," or use cold logic in refusing to deal with hot emotions.

If both partners are withdrawers, a marriage's growth and intimacy are in great danger. If both are confronters, heads may roll! The ideal seems to be to have one confronter and one withdrawer with *both* being willing to learn from the personality of the other. The confronter needs to learn timing, peacemaking, and tact. The withdrawer needs to learn honesty, the ability to share feelings, and discipline to face issues as they come up.

Why? In order to obey God. God tells us to "speak the truth in love" (Ephesians 4:15), which is both an admonition to unloving confronters to speak in *love*, and also a command to withdrawers to *speak*.

Scripture abounds in instructions concerning conflict, such as "faithful are the wounds of a friend" (Proverbs 27:6, NASB); "admonish one another with all wisdom" (Colossians 3:16); "keep short accounts" (that's my translation of Ecclesiastes 8:11, "When the sentence for a crime is not quickly carried out, the hearts of the people are filled with schemes to do wrong"); and "If your brother sins against you, go and show him his fault" (Matthew 18:15). These commands for *all* Christians are especially necessary between husbands and wives.

Some "Remembers" Before You Start

Whether we are withdrawers or confronters, God has established some rules for our behavior in the midst of conflict. Let me suggest a study in the book of Proverbs to find your own list, but here are a few principles from *The Living Bible* to start you off. Review these "remembers" from Proverbs to prepare yourself when you know you're heading into a conflict situation:

Remember to keep cool. Someone has said that emotions have to be cooled until the fight takes the form of a problem to be solved. As Proverbs puts it: "A fool is quick-tempered; a wise man stays cool when insulted" (12:16).

Remember to lower your voice instead of raising it. "A soft answer turns away wrath, but harsh words cause quarrels" (15:1).

Remember to think before you speak. "Self-control means controlling the tongue! A quick retort can ruin everything" (13:3).

Remember to be kind and humble. "Pride leads to arguments; be humble, take advice and become wise" (13:10).

Both withdrawers and confronters need godly maturity to avoid trying to "win" a battle. Confronters want to win by overpowering the other person; yet God would not have us be guilty of either power-grabbing or character assassination. Withdrawers want to win by silence. Not only must we be careful of our motive in a conflict, but we must avoid arguments that are not allowed to *end*.

Just What Is the Problem, Anyway?

Now we move from *approaching* the conflict to *identifying* the conflict. Have you, as a couple, ever put down on paper what your conflicts are actually about—by subject matter? For instance, are the majority of your fights about irritating habits, discipline of children, money, in-laws, sex, unmet needs, religion, vacations, use of time, and so on?

Jack and I are convinced that a great percentage of conflicts are not *real* conflicts at all, but a matter of misunderstanding. A husband asks if his wife has a new dress on, thinking it looks great, but she interprets the question as saying she's spent too much money. And away we go.

Another large percentage of conflicts come under the "hidden agenda" kind of fight that requires patience and multiple attempts to find the way beneath the surface to the *real* issue—an issue of which even the person beginning it may be unaware. A wife picks a fight because her husband forgot to take out the garbage, but the real issue is her desire for more physical affection. In fact, the desire for more love and affection is probably the number one problem beneath the surface of many quarrels. Years ago, one older wife observed profoundly, "I wish men would realize that many times when wives are unhappy, irritable, or ready to pick a fight, they really need a reassurance of their husband's love." After years of observation, I'd say she was right on.

I still have difficulty at times telling Jack in a direct way what I'm feeling or needing. Because, after all, to *tell* him that I need a hug would somehow take away from its effectiveness. To *tell* him that I need more time talking in depth would reveal that my need is greater than his, and that—horrible thought!—I need him more than he needs me. And so I withdraw and puff on my need with little hurting breaths until Jack becomes aware of my gloom and asks me what is the matter. Or some *unrelated* argument starts and the whole smelly pot boils over.

Then even when he asks me, I will likely give a vague and irrelevant answer—also unfair. Instead of stating my needs directly— "Honey, I'm really feeling like the whole world is trying to shoot me down and I need you to hold me for a few minutes"—I just hint at them—"Oh, it's been a terrible day, but I'll be okay." I want Jack to *know* what I need without me telling him because to tell him is a bit humiliating or embarrassing. Many wives excel in this little game of "He should know what I mean or need."

I've also been guilty of stating a request in a negative rather than the positive form. I might say, "I haven't left the house all day," rather than "Would you mind watching the children for thirty minutes so I can take a walk?" Or "I don't have anything in the house for dinner," instead of saying, "Honey, do you suppose we could go out for a bite to eat tonight?"

Identifying the *real* problem when conflict arises is a crucial step toward resolution. Here is a series of steps that we've found helpful:

Define the problem or issue of disagreement. Sometimes this step can get complicated. Often a couple doesn't get to the real issue on the first go-round. A prior step could be taking it individually to the Lord and praying for His wisdom to define the dispute specifically. James 1:5 states, "If any of you lacks wisdom, he should ask God, who gives generously to all without finding fault, and it will be given to him."

Some will find it helpful to write their thoughts out on paper after they've prayed, and go through several sessions of thinking and praying before they are able to define the true difficulty.

Agreeing on the precise nature of the disagreement may take several sessions as well. But stick with it until you both agree on the exact issue.

How does each of you contribute to the problem? Be as honest as you can about your Unwanted Repetitive Patterns here. Own up to any unfair techniques.

Brainstorm and list all possible solutions. Be creative on this, and don't ridicule even the craziest ideas. What could each of you do differently the next time to avoid repeating this same problem?

Discuss each solution and agree on one to try. Make sure you're both clear on what the change will be and how expectations need to be adjusted accordingly. Agree on how each person will work toward the solution.

Set a time to review your progress. If you haven't hit upon the perfect solution the first time, try another of your solutions or go back to step three and try again. But of course, the whole thing breaks down if you aren't willing to come to grips with the basic issue that is causing the conflict in the first place.

Many marriage counselors believe that, except in rare instances, the specific complaint named by squabbling partners is merely a symptom of a deeper conflict between them. Obviously, unless a couple understands what they are fighting about and are willing to deal with the underlying cause, their arguments will continue.

But sometimes the underlying cause is so deeply buried, it's not evident—at least on the conscious level. Some heart-searching questions may need to be asked . . . before God. Begin by praying Psalm 139:23-24, "Search me, O God, and know my heart; test me and know my anxious thoughts. See if there is any offensive way in me, and lead me in the way everlasting." Isn't that terrific? God really can help us know ourselves. He can reveal *me* to me!

One of the first questions I need to ask Him is about that "underlying cause." Exactly *why* am I so furious? What is the true issue here?

A primary factor may involve *control* issues. Ask yourself, "Am I irritable and quarrelsome because I need to feel in *control* of our relationship in some way?" This is a factor more often than we might like to admit. Sometimes when a wife goes back to work, for instance, a husband subconsciously feels threatened and starts to pick at things he never did before simply because he feels he's lost control.

A second question to ask of the Lord in discerning root issues concerns *attitude*—about life, my partner, my marriage. Am I focusing attention on the problems in our relationship and neglecting the positive factors that brought us together?

A third diagnostic question could be, "Is this a time of crisis that is putting extra pressure on our relationship?" Some areas of conflict are to be expected at certain stages in the marital lifecycle—such as a new baby, a move, a death in the family, loss of a job, or health problems.

There may be times when we need the guidance of a marriage counselor, a pastor, or an older Christian to help us uncover the root cause of repeated quarrels. Proverbs urges us to use godly counsel. A mature couple will go for needed help quickly. Books can be helpful if we make the effort to read them, preferably aloud together, sorting through what the real issues are.

How Do We Handle It?

Now let's move from *identifying* conflict to *handling* conflict. Here are some overall guidelines:

Focus on the beautiful. Whole books have been written about thinking positively, but the Bible says it best: "Finally, brothers, whatever is true, whatever is noble, whatever is right, whatever is pure, whatever is lovely, whatever is admirable—if anything is excellent or praiseworthy—think about such things" (Philippians 4:8). But what do you and I give our attention to? Usually, what we'd like to see changed, what we don't like, and those things that don't please us.

Scripture makes it clear that we become what we think about. Think negatively, and you become a negative person.

Try listing all the wonderful qualities you appreciate in your spouse—whatever made you fall in love in the first place. Read the list every day and add to it. Pick one quality to share with your partner daily with a special compliment. Use your list for a "Thank You, God" prayer time. Talk with your spouse about the pleasures you've shared during your marriage, the mutual goals you wish to reach.

Refuse to "win" an argument. "Winning" is really losing because you haven't broken through to better understanding of each other and the situation.

Learn to communicate ideas and feelings more clearly. Work at the art of dialogue until you can explain to the other's satisfaction what *the other one* is feeling and saying. Or you might try "role reversal"—switch sides in arguments, or do each other's chores for a while so you can understand what your partner contends with on a daily basis.

Be very careful about venting hostile feelings. "Letting it all hang out" usually just increases both persons' anger and aggravates the problem that triggered it. It seldom helps a couple come to grips intelligently with the basic reason for their fight.

Study your partner's differences. Learn from these, respect them.

Never underestimate the power of praying together. God really is in the business of answering prayer. He can break through our stubborn spirits if we give Him the opportunity. I know it's hard to invite Him in when a quarrel is in process, but if we will do it, He will surprise us with joy and forgiveness.

And remember, you can't change anyone. Only God can. Openness to God's changes in our *own* lives is vital. Someone has said, "The greatest prayer you can pray in marriage is, 'Lord, change this marriage, beginning with *me.*'"

Make physical contact. One counselor suggests you face each other when you quarrel with knees touching, holding hands. Hard to shout, exaggerate, and accuse in that position, isn't it?

Forgive. Ah, that's a tough one, isn't it? But God's unconditional

forgiveness to us is the basis of His command to forgive others uncon-
ditionally. We are to forgive over and over again; before we pray; when
the other repents; for the sake of Christ and to defeat Satan; as Christ
forgave us; and with a heart of love.[3]

Go beyond forgiveness to understanding. Stay with the argument—or come back to it as much as needed when the emotions
have subsided somewhat—until you both understand from the other's
point of view *why* it happened. Perhaps it was just a bad mood that
happens occasionally to all of us, but knowing and understanding the
effect of a mood on your spouse is also valuable. Keep exploring until
the *good* aspects of those differences have been discovered.

Don't waste a good fight! You can grow by determining to use
conflict to know your spouse. To understand, to adjust, to change.
And finally to *accept* that person God gave you in order to sharpen
one another and be conformed to the image of Jesus Christ.

Learn to Be Resolvers

In review of this in-depth look at confronters and withdrawers in conflict, let's emphasize the goal of *resolving*. To that end, we present "The
Five Rs":

1. *Repeat* to each other what the quarrel is really about.
Write it out if necessary, redefining it until both of you agree.
This in itself will resolve a good many arguments.

2. *Release* it to God in prayer—separately and together. It is
difficult to stay angry when you are taking it to the Lord.

3. *Reason* it through together. Use the five steps we listed
in this chapter as a guide for identifying the problem as well as
possible solutions.

4. *Resolve* and *leave* it. When it's over, move beyond it.
Admit your mistakes, learn from criticism, and start fresh.

5. *Rebuild* the relationship afterwards. "Love forgets mistakes; nagging about them parts the best of friends" (Proverbs
17:9, TLB).

If your partner is unwilling to work toward a solution, some of
these steps will still help—defining the difficulty, praying about it,
forgiving even when the other hasn't asked forgiveness. Ask God for

His wisdom on timing—when or if to bring it up again, what the next step is, what you alone can do to improve the situation and continue building the relationship in other areas. Above all, ask for wisdom in knowing when to speak and when to be still, for discerning if the issue should be forced into the open or put behind you unresolved.

If both of you are willing to work at conflict resolution, then you are ready to learn how to turn every argument into a *discussion*. And boy, is that hard!

To fight—that's okay.

To fight fairly—that's growth.

But to fight with kindness and love—that's grace!

NOTES:

1. Norma Peterson, "How to Stop Fighting and Start Loving Again," *McCalls* (August 1983), page 8.
2. Chuck and Barb Snyder, *Incompatibility: Grounds for a Great Marriage* (Sisters, OR: Questar Publishers, 1988), page 115.
3. Matthew 18:21, Mark 11:25-26, Luke 17:3-4, 2 Corinthians 2:10, Ephesians 4:32, Colossians 3:13.

PART IV

THE WAY WE ACT

16

Should It Be Done Right, or Right Now?

PERFECTIONIST VS. NON-PERFECTIONIST

JACK

We pulled up in front of the small repair garage and parked our rental car. The lock on the back door of this station wagon was jammed and for two days, I'd had to climb over the back seat for suitcases and golf clubs. So here we were at a garage recommended by our hotel manager, impatient to continue our week-long holiday in Scotland on this beautiful day.

After finding out that the repairs would take about half an hour, Carole wandered across the street to explore the ruins of a beautiful old abbey.

When she came back, the door was fixed and I was busy straightening out the mess in the rear of the car. She looked at what I was doing and asked, "Why don't you leave that till later?"

Irritated at her "why" question, I replied firmly, "Because I want to straighten it out *now*."

"Well, don't get mad at me."

"Well, you always argue with me," I said defensively.

Now at this time, Carole and I had been married thirty-five years! In fact, that trip was a celebration of our thirty-fifth anniversary. Yet in just four sentences, we violated three rules of good relationship. (You have to work hard to do that!)

First, Carole asked a threatening "why" question. Second, I used the inflammatory "always"—unwise at best, and obviously not true. Few of us human beings are consistent enough for "always" and "never" to describe our actions. Third, we had failed (again) to understand how different we are.

For the next ten minutes in the car, things were extremely quiet. Then Carole began to chuckle and so did I. We were laughing at ourselves and the dumb stunt we'd just pulled. We apologized to each other, talked it through, and proceeded to have a wonderful day.

Fifteen or twenty years ago, it probably would have taken us the whole day to resolve the conflict arising from that four-sentence exchange. But God has taught us some things in the intervening years—about being open in sharing our feelings quickly, not sulking, and forgiving quickly. But another important factor we have discovered is not to *stop* with forgiving, but to use the conflict to learn about ourselves and each other.

What had happened here? What was the core reason for our squabble? As we talked, we realized that the fundamental cause of the heated dispute hinged on the *reason* I was carefully straightening out the suitcases and golf clubs.

The fact of the matter is that I tend to be a perfectionist, and Carole is not. I wouldn't call Carole sloppy; but Carole is, well, *fast*.

From my point of view, the logical, necessary thing to do after the back door of the station wagon was fixed was to get the mess cleaned up—in an orderly fashion.

But what did Carole want to do when she came back from her exploration of the abbey? Why, she wanted to *get going*, of course. We'd already wasted half an hour, and all of Scotland lay before us!

Now we *knew* this characteristic about each other; we just *forgot* it for a moment and so didn't apply our understanding to that particular situation—or we would have been more considerate and accepting on that lovely morning.

When Carole and I first got married, we were one hundred and eighty degrees apart on this one. But over the years, we've adjusted and changed and now we are apart, oh, maybe twenty degrees or so. That *may* be all the progress we're going to make in this lifetime. But still, that's a lot of progress!

Of course, there are still some things we don't do together because of this difference. For instance, we don't wash a car together.

Can you picture that? Carole has her bucket and sponge and I have my bucket and sponge and we begin on each side of the car. *Whish, whish, whish* and three minutes later Carole says "I'm finished" while I'm still working on the front fender. I look up in amazement and go around to inspect her side. Then I make some dumb statement like, "You call that *finished*?" (It's a wonder I haven't gotten a bucket of water over my head!)

We don't hang wallpaper together. I insist on the lines being straight up and down. Enough said on that one.

A perfectionist, it's said, takes great pains and gives them to everyone else. And I must admit, I now feel sorry for those who have to live with a rigid and extreme perfectionist.

CAROLE

Perfectionists mystify me. Non-perfectionists just stand and shake their heads in disbelief at some things perfectionists do. Things like:

- using two napkins for meals—a cloth one for their lap and a paper one to wipe their hands on.

- keeping separate dish towels for glassware, dishes, pans.

- hanging shirts or blouses by sleeve length, color coordinated, facing forward, hangers all in one direction.

Now I admire many things about a perfectionist. I know one lady who is past her ninetieth birthday but still looks at all times as though she just stepped out of a fashion magazine. Even her robe and slippers match. She spends time searching for the precise shade of earrings, shoes, purse, or blouse to create the perfect combination. I admire that *greatly*. (And sometimes I even work on it!) But it is simply not a big priority for me. My purse and shoes rarely match because I stay with one neutral-color purse. It simply takes too much time to change purses for every outfit. If my shoes and jewelry go with my suit, it's only because it was just as fast to put on the matching ones.

I can clean my house in two and a half hours (now you *know* I can't move the furniture in that amount of time, or wash windows). I can fix dinner in twenty minutes, wash the car in fifteen—or less. I go for the fastest, easiest way to do things. So I *don't* hang my clothes out on the line to air-freshen them. I don't iron anything I don't have to, and my garden takes minimum upkeep.

Of course, as in every characteristic we've talked about, great inconsistencies abound. If a picture is crooked, I have to straighten it (if I have time). The chrome on the kitchen sink may need shining, but the counter must be wiped clean (if I have time). The dining room table needs refinishing and is ignored (I don't have time!). However, it bothers me if the towels in the bathroom aren't folded twice and precisely centered (and I make time!).

Inconsistent? Yes. But as one sage observed, the only consistent thing in this world is that we are inconsistent.

Behold Jack, the perfectionist, who wants a picture light placed in such a way that the cord goes into the wall and not down the outside even if it means a major electrical job. The overhead fan must be exactly centered, the wallpaper perfectly hung. His undershirts are meticulously folded and stacked neatly in the drawer.

But his desk is cluttered (and I don't dare touch it because he knows exactly where things are) and his tools in the basement haven't been organized for years.

Perhaps the secret is not only to understand in *general* our various traits and characteristics, but also to know thoroughly our particular exceptions and those of our marriage partner.

We probably also need to know the drawbacks of being quick-and-easy versus perfectionistic. For me, one of the major liabilities of being a fast person is that I want things done *right now* and I want others to be ready to do and go *right now* too.

I remember well, though it happened years ago, an episode while we were on a trip with Jack's parents to the New York World's Fair. Mom Mayhall, who is an absolute dear but a perfectionist, usually had one more thing to do when *my* schedule said we were to leave for the day. So I began "managing" (a nice term for nagging), making suggestions to all concerned such as, "Don't forget, we leave at eight a.m." . . . "You will be ready at eight, won't you?" . . . and finally, "MOM, are you ready to leave?"

One night Jack told me in no uncertain terms to "stop it!" And I hadn't even realized I was doing it!

I was crushed. I also felt helpless as I realized this characteristic of bossiness, brought on by being so "fast," had become an ingrained habit I was unaware of. I cried and prayed all night. I felt that even though Jack had to *love* me (he was my husband, right?), he probably didn't *like* me.

It took me three days of saying scarcely *anything* for fear I'd say the wrong thing, to finally get God's perspective on it. I begged God to change me, but realized that I needed Him first to make me aware of what I was doing and then to change me from the inside. Not just my deliberate actions, though I needed to change them too, but my *inner* gentleness.

God is not finished with me yet on this one. And it helped to realize that it wasn't a matter of Jack not liking me. He was really trying to help me in this thing.

Sometimes we can even laugh over this difference now.

I loved this story I read recently: A couple were discussing the wallpaper they had just hung. Don was annoyed at Debby's indifference to what he felt was a poor job. "The problem is that I'm a perfectionist and you're not," he finally said to her.

"Exactly!" she replied. "That's why you married me and I married you!"[1]

JACK

Perfectionists just stand and shake their heads in disbelief at some things that non-perfectionists do:

- rush through tasks so fast they have to be done over again—and sometimes again, and again.

- drop things, spill things, break things because they're in such a hurry.

- settle for just getting things *done* rather than getting them done *right* (whether it is washing a car, hanging wallpaper, or weeding the garden).

Which words describe a perfectionist? Correct, precise, orderly, neat, careful. They want to *do it right*.

Describe a non-perfectionist? Use these phrases: "let's go!"; "never mind"; "it's okay"; "don't worry." They want to *do it now*.

My mother gave us a colorful windsock for Christmas a year ago. Because it was a bit too long for one part of the patio, we temporarily put it away. Then one day last summer when Mom was coming for a visit, I saw Carole out on the patio reaching up as far as she could at the edge of the deck to hammer a nail onto a beam. Soon the windsock was blowing gently in the wind.

The next morning the windsock was lying on the deck. It had blown off the nail, of course, in a stronger wind that night.

Still in my pajamas, I got an enclosed bracket, a ladder, measured the exact place the sock should hang, and put it up the right way. But to my critical eye, I thought the sock was a bit long even for that part of the patio. (Perfectionists tend to be critical, did you know that?)

But I guess if Carole hadn't hung it *wrong*, I wouldn't have hung it *right*! Fortunately, God knew what He was doing when He chose Carole and me for each other. If I had married my own type, would anything ever get done? And if Carole had married her own type, would anything get done *well*? I'm so grateful He led us together.

How to Complete, Not Compete

How important it is to look at the positives in this particular difference. If you don't, you may go a little nuts!

I admit there have been times when I've been irritated because of missing socks, pink shorts (because something red got mixed in with the white wash), collars that wouldn't lay right because of being pressed hurriedly. But what a bonus it is that I rarely have to *wait* for Carole! She is usually ready to go before I am. She entertains easily because she isn't insistent that the house or the meal be perfect. She isn't an uptight person and accepts herself and others readily. Friends, those are things to be thankful for.

On the other hand, Carole appreciates the fact that I do things carefully. She rarely needs to get involved in our travel plans—and we travel over fifty percent of the time. She knows I'll carefully investigate the best prices for rental cars, hotels, and get the needed receipts. I keep the books, including balancing the checkbook. And I've even learned to be patient (most of the time) when Carole copies the amount of the check incorrectly or subtracts the amount wrong and so the balance is a few cents off at the end of the month. She tries. She just does it so quickly that she sometimes makes mistakes.

But aren't you glad that some people are perfectionists? How would you like a non-perfectionist dentist, doctor, engineer, or tailor? And aren't you glad there are fast people? Think of perfectionistic artists who would never be satisfied with what they wrote or painted—and so they'd keep their art to themselves rather than let others enjoy it. Or perfectionistic people managers, who would demand so much of their team that "good" would never be "good enough."

It is critical that we allow the sharpening process in one another's lives to take place in this area. I'm much easier to work for and live with, and much more accepting of myself and others, because I've lived with Carole all these years. And she has slowed down in some things, taking time to do them right the first time. She has learned to organize, set priorities, and select the important over the inconsequential much more often than when we first married.

We need each other.

We learn from each other.

And I kid you not, it's fun to be married to each other. Honestly: the delight is not only in the ways we are alike, but in the differences as well.

NOTE:
1. "Life in These United States," by B.N.M. of Chicago, *Readers Digest* (May 1988), page 113.

You Step Forward,
I Step Back
AGGRESSIVE VS. TIMID

JACK

The steakhouse came highly recommended. After we eased into a booth, I placed our order confidently: "We'll have the filets—medium, please."

Fifteen minutes later, the waiter placed our steaks before us. I could see the blood running even before I took an investigative cut. "This steak is too rare," I declared.

"Sweetheart," Carole murmured, "why don't you trade with me? I don't mind it cooked that way."

"Yes, you do," I countered and glanced at her plate. "And anyway, yours is rare too." I raised my hand in a futile attempt to attract the waiter's attention.

"Let's not make a fuss," Carole begged. "Can't we just ignore it and enjoy the evening?"

"Hey, we're paying good money for this steak. I'm going to send them both back," I insisted and succeeded this time in summoning our waiter.

We waited another fifteen minutes before our steaks appeared again. As I cut into them, I groaned. "Oh, no, now they're cooked to death! No way are they *medium*."

Carole chided, "Well, they were probably upset that you sent them back."

"That's *their* problem," I retorted.

147

Once again I called the waiter as Carole tried to disappear under the tablecloth. And finally our steaks were served—*medium*. But I don't think Carole enjoyed hers very much.

I'm sure most of you have either participated in or witnessed such a scenario. And you've either cheered or been embarrassed by it, depending upon your nature.

The characteristic of assertiveness is called by many names. If you and I are both assertive, I might call *you* hostile; but me? Well, I'm forceful. I'll name you belligerent; me, enterprising. The other person is pugnacious, but I'm energetic. That one is contentious, but I am zealous. (Would you believe that all of these are synonyms of the word "assertive" in my *thesaurus*?)

Sometimes this characteristic leads to embarrassing conclusions. This story appeared in the *Vail Trail's Pastimes*:

Dan Mulrooney, owner of Bart and Yeti's, tells the story of an impatient patron who, seeing that all the tables were filled and after being told that there would be an hour wait, demanded to see Bart. "I'm a close personal friend of Bart's and I want to see him. He'll get me a table."

The bar, of course, was named after two dogs.

So Mulrooney said, "You're a close personal friend of his, huh?"

The would-be patron insisted he was.

"He's kind of busy," Mulrooney said, "but since you're such a close friend of his, I'll get him."

Leading the dog to the hostess stand, Mulrooney said, "This is Bart, see if he can get you a table."

The man decided against dinner at Bart and Yeti's.[1]

So much for assertiveness!

On the other hand, if I am the opposite of assertive, I may call timidity a number of things as well. I may say you're fainthearted, but I'm humble. I call him fearful; myself, retiring. She is wishy-washy; I am a peacemaker.

The many names for assertiveness and timidity indicate the many and varied aspects of these traits. Obviously, there are both negative and positive sides to each.

The positive side of forceful people's character is that they take charge when necessary and are usually outspoken on behalf of others as well as themselves.

The negative counterpart may be that they tend to be rigid, very control-oriented, and perhaps belligerent. They can also be overly independent to the point of not asking for help—such as being lost but not stopping to ask directions. More serious is that many people who have this characteristic hesitate to go for counseling until a major disaster or crisis has already occurred.

The positive side of compliant people is that they tend to be peacemakers, polite, and easy on others or themselves. On the negative side, they may be indecisive, and in their desire not to ruffle anyone's feathers, they can act out of weakness rather than on firm convictions.

At first glance, this difference doesn't seem to be a big deal. But it can be! When the self-assured partner overwhelms and rides over the timid one, when daily situations cause embarrassment or loss of respect, or when either tendency is carried to an extreme, then it can loom large in a relationship.

CAROLE

I'm sure there are people who need "assertiveness training." I probably need to take a course in it one of these days. I'm the kind of person who doesn't like to return things to a store (I'd sooner be out the money); I'll wriggle out of making unpleasant phone calls if I possibly can; I'd rarely ask for a different table at a restaurant or return food not cooked well; I'd rather wipe dirty silverware with my napkin than ask the waitress for replacements; I won't speak to a smoker in a non-smoking section (though I'm getting better at this one). If someone shouts at me, I'm inclined to withdraw—or cry—rather than speak back firmly (I'd *rarely* shout back). I'm not sure if my peace-at-any-price attitude is based on fear or on wanting to keep the situation as calm and peaceful as possible.

Regardless of motive, to me the enjoyment of time together is much more important than how my eggs are cooked. If rectifying a situation is necessary, then I want it done quietly and pleasantly, without threat to the pleasure of companionship.

Assertiveness often turns into negative aggressiveness. I've seen people, in the name of standing up for rights, get belligerent, impolite, and unkind. Perhaps assertiveness training should be followed up by a course on manners. Nevertheless, if I didn't have Jack, I would need Assertiveness Training 101 because it is often exactly the trait needed in some situations.

Perhaps a naturally forceful person has the potential for leading. Or it could be he is a born "thinker" and comes up with ideas along with the drive to put them into practice. Whatever is involved, I'm glad I married a person who is always thinking and isn't afraid to speak up about his good ideas. On one occasion in particular I had opportunity to be *very* grateful for Jack's refusal to back off when events didn't turn out the way we'd expected.

Our daughter and her husband were in language school in Costa Rica, and we were making a trip to visit them. We had been speaking at a conference center in Tennessee, and so our flight plan was Chattanooga-Atlanta, Atlanta-Miami, and Miami-Costa Rica, then returning through Venezuela to visit missionaries there. We had saved a great deal of money by purchasing an advance ticket that could not be changed in any way.

The night before our departure, we had dinner in Chattanooga with friends, told the clerk at our motel near the airport we would need a ride to the terminal at 6:45 a.m. for an 8:00 a.m. flight, and retired early. (Of course, I kept waking up to check the time and make sure we would hear the alarm.)

We arrived with our luggage at the front desk next morning at 6:45. The same clerk who had been on duty the night before said, "You're running a bit late, aren't you?" to which we replied, "Why, no. It's 6:45."

She replied, "No, it's 7:45!"

We were horrified to discover that seven miles out of Chattanooga, the time zone changed! Not once during dinner or at the motel had we seen a clock with local time.

We made a mad dash to the airport but were greeted with the sight of our plane taking off. We had missed the first lap of our trip to Costa Rica with no apparent way to catch up to our Atlanta-Miami flight.

I was sick at heart and sick to my stomach!

But my dear husband is *always thinking*. A car rental was out—the drive was too long to make our flight out of Atlanta. To break into our "excursion ticket" would have cost about five hundred dollars each—a thousand dollars we didn't have. As we prayed, Jack asked the airline ticket agent, "What about chartering a plane to Atlanta?" The agent's face lit up as he said, "It would cost you one hundred and sixty dollars, but that's certainly less than a new ticket."

In twenty minutes we were at a small hanger, our luggage stowed in a plane all ready to take off. But the pilot didn't show up! We waited for him until it was too late to catch our *next* lap in Atlanta. I was fighting tears. But Jack's mind kept buzzing as he prayed and I worried (I knew even then that what he did was more effective).

When the pilot finally came, our only alternative seemed to be to cancel everything and wait until the next day. However, not only would that have cost us the thousand dollars, but we had no way to contact our loved ones who were waiting in Costa Rica.

Jack kept thinking. He discovered another flight that could make our Miami-Costa Rica connection, and off we went in a little four-seater to Atlanta. A shuttle-bus whisked us to the gate fifteen minutes before departure.

But when the agent at the counter looked at our tickets, she said, "I can't let you on this plane without rewriting your whole ticket, and I don't have time to do that before the plane leaves."

My heart seemed to drop right through the floor.

Jack's assertiveness came to the fore. "Lady," he said firmly, "you've *got* to get us on that plane. There *must* be a way you can help us." She hesitated and then said, "Well, I could let you go on standby and then we wouldn't have to rewrite your ticket."

The plane had plenty of room, so we went standby and finally caught up with our originally-planned flight in Miami. I didn't take a relaxed breath, however, until we were on the Miami-Costa Rica lap of the trip. Then I thanked God fervently for working things out *and* for my ever-thinking assertive husband. And I felt sorry for all the couples in the world who are both nonassertive. I guess in those cases, one would have to pray and work extra-hard at *learning* to keep thinking, to keep pressing, to keep insisting.

Perhaps nonassertive people are more likely to be worriers. Even though I am by nature optimistic, sometimes negative ideas and thoughts plague me: "We're late, so they probably won't hold our reservations"; "What if we get lost? We'll never find our way back"; "We need to leave a detailed itinerary in case something happens."

Part of that, I suppose, is my mind for the details along with my concern for the "what if's" of life. But part of it may be that I tend to feel the situation controls me instead of my having the ability to control the situation.

Now I *have* learned to force myself to do things I might not be inclined to do. I can confront if I have to. In fact, sometimes in my need for unclouded relationships, I confront when Jack might want to let it go—not if it has to do with the two of us, but sometimes with other people.

So in situations involving interpersonal relationships, I may be the assertive one. In almost all other situations, Jack takes that responsibility—and much more naturally than I do. In all honesty, I depend on him to take charge aggressively when I'm either at a total loss for words or just naturally reticent.

I need him. He needs me. And we all need to be needed, don't we?

A poem by Harold L. Myra begins,

We lie in the bed together,
backs of our heads on pillows,
resting easy.
But something troubles you.

"You don't need me,"
you say into the air and at me.
"You don't need me like I need you."
I turn my head toward you, and you add,
"You'd get along fine without me.
"Wouldn't you?"

What aching words: "You don't need me."

But in marriage, the fact is that we do. The aggressive individual needs the caution of the peacemaker. The timid needs the bold. The forceful "I'm going to win" person needs another to warn him about breaking relationships and to remind him of the importance of understanding over winning. Yet the peace-at-any-price personality needs the confronter to emphasize that she can't resolve issues by avoiding them.

God created them both.

May our differences become links within unbreakable chains forged by God Himself, hammered out on the anvil of the everydayness of living . . . and loving.

Together.

NOTES:
1. Quoted from *The Vail Trail's Pastimes* (August 26, 1988), page 12.
2. Part of a poem by Harold L. Myra, *Partnership* (January-February 1988), page 26.

18

But Seriously...
Are You Kidding?
SERIOUS & RESOLUTE VS.
CASUAL & RELAXED

JACK

Lawnmowers have personalities. Really.

There's the phlegmatic mower. It starts slow and proceeds with a steady chug-a-lug.

Our neighbor owns a sanguine machine that roars into life and chews up the grass with such enthusiasm it drowns out all conversation on our back porch.

Mine? It's a melancholic with highs and lows and sometimes creative ideas of its own. I have to admit that sometimes I wish it were a choleric grass-cutter—though if it were, it might get too hot or go so hard I couldn't run fast enough to stay up with it.

It could be that people should be matched up with the temperament of their lawnmowers. But then you'd have to sort through a whale of a lot of factors.

Observe people at a football game. One red-faced man is shouting himself hoarse while his wife, wrapped in a blanket, sits stoically by his side.

Catch a glimpse of them at an old sentimental movie as one tears through a box of tissues and the other looks on dispassionate and dry-eyed.

Notice them in a shopping mall—one strides resolutely along, obviously intent on buying a specific item, while the other—with nonstop commentary—dawdles along behind, looking enthusiastically-into each window.

Look closely when they attend a meeting. One sits knitting quietly, eyes on a half-finished sweater. The other hangs on every word of the speaker, laughs uproariously at the stories, and nods at each well-taken point.

So what if your partner plods as you proceed in jerks and bumps? What does it matter that you like the whipped cream and cotton candy of life and your spouse always goes for the meat and potatoes?

If being out of step with your spouse never irritates you, then skip this chapter. But if at times you grit your teeth to stop from screaming when he is so doggone *serious* and you want to whoop it up, or she laughs when you know it's no laughing matter, or his goals are so set in cement that you can't blast them out with TNT while you prefer to recline in your La-Z-Boy until two hours before the decision point . . . then read on.

Actually, it's difficult to describe in a few well-chosen words this difference in the way we respond to life. Some call it a "high D" (for "dominant") as opposed to a "low C" (for "compliant"). Others opt for the sanguine, choleric, melancholic, or phlegmatic labels. Still others look for its definition in motivational profiles. But whatever we name it, it is critical that we understand that some people are born *serious* while others seem destined to have a casual, lighthearted, and relaxed attitude concerning life itself.

The pace, concentration, and attitudes of the two are different. One is care*ful* and the other care*free* (and the careful person might say care*less*).

This personality trait and approach to life pops up so often that when these opposites marry, each is frequently thrown off-balance by the attitude of the spouse. And probably *especially* in this trait, one can be judged *wrong* instead of merely *different*. If extreme, this one may really *be* wrong.

But let's dissect these approaches in a couple of critical areas.

The first area, and one of the most common, is the realm of *discipline*.

Shortly after Bob came to know Christ a number of years ago, he learned the importance of having a few minutes with God each morning to help him grow in his newfound Christian life. In spite of an incredibly busy schedule, I don't think Bob has missed a morning.

That's great. The difficulty is he cannot for the life of him understand that his wife has struggled for *years* to have a consistent time with the Lord. The way Bob is made up, if you should do it, then you just *do* it. Excuses are not acceptable.

Bob is disciplined in every area of his life. Self-discipline is not a problem with him—not in his weight, nor in his schedule, nor in his spiritual life. This makes it hard for him to understand why others have difficulty in this area. He needs to recognize his wife's efforts in the context of *her* orientation, not his.

Psychologists tell us that the three things people argue most about are communication, sex, and money. In our observation, a close fourth is the area of disciplining children.

In the how, when, and what (and even where and why) of disciplining our offspring, I'm sure we are influenced much by our own upbringing, observation of those close to us, books we read, and the study of the Bible. But somewhere enmeshed in it all is simply the way we are as *people*. Some of us are born disciplinarians. At four years old, we were probably turning a baleful eye on our younger sibling and saying, "But Mother *said.* . . ."

Others wish to leave the discipline to someone else and long to give children only warm fuzzies and love—to be their kid's "best pal." But some "pals" won't accept any responsibility for their children's training, which frustrates the serious authoritarian no end. Relaxed personalities may be *too* relaxed concerning discipline both of children and of themselves.

Although contrasting approaches to discipline may create major rifts in a marriage, even more critical can be the way various personalities view *sin*.

CAROLE

She was probably in her forties, but at a distance, she could have been mistaken for a teenager: slim, thick shoulder-length dark hair, attractive. But as we drove past the rich farmland of the Midwest, her face was lined with pain. Her husband had had a brief affair. It was over. He'd said he was sorry and had asked forgiveness.

But it wasn't that easy for her. And when she was moody, when she wanted extra assurance of his love, when she asked for needed time for the trust to be rebuilt, his answer was, "I *said* I was sorry. Why can't you forget it?"

We've heard similar scenarios over and over.

Before we discuss a personality type that views this situation as casual, we need to explore a definite male-female difference.

Those who have studied the subject tell us that to most men, sex is an act, an interlude in time. Some men separate love from the act of sex and because of this, they do not consider an affair—whether a one-night stand or a few-months' entanglement—as deep a betrayal as do their wives.

For most women, however, sex and love are interwoven so deeply that it is inconceivable for them to think of sex as just another bodily function. So if the husband has been unfaithful, to her it is a sure sign that he doesn't love her—or at least love her *enough*. It is more than a broken trust. It is a tearing down of all that has been built up over the years—the respect and the love, as well as the trust.

To many men, adultery is something to regret. To most women, adultery seems to smash their whole lives beyond repair.

So a man says, "I'm sorry." And a woman's heart screams, "Sorry? Those are empty words when my heart is broken, my life shattered, and my trust destroyed!"

A woman may forgive—certainly has to forgive. But for her, the love must be fanned into flame all over again. The trust must be built from nothing once more. The respect must be laboriously reconstructed. And this takes time—not just weeks, but months, perhaps even years. A husband must be aware of the need to woo her, win her, and help her build that trust all over again.

So part of the way adultery is viewed could be the way a man views sex.

JACK

Another part of it could be personality type. If a husband is a laid-back, easy-on-himself personality, a don't-make-waves kind of person, then his attitude toward sin and forgiveness could be affected by his attitude toward *life*. If he doesn't take anything seriously, he may not take sin seriously either.

But here we draw the line. In this issue, we can no longer say "it's different." We've got to say "it's *wrong*."

Our view concerning sin is partly determined by our background, our depth as Christians, our knowledge of the holiness of God, the example of our parents, the teaching of our church, and our attitude and approach to life. But make no mistake: Even if we have an easygoing personality, we cannot be casual about sin, or the importance of forgiving and being forgiven, or right and wrong, or the need for deep and true repentance.

Why? Because God says sin is a serious matter. To take sin lightly, no matter what our personality, is wrong. A number of times, God's Word tells us to be serious about life; to be "sober" in our approach to our years; to "gird your minds for action, keep sober in spirit" (1 Peter 1:13, NASB).

That sober attitude doesn't change my personality type or my approach to life. It is simply obedience to God. It's asking God to change whatever in my life does not line up to His Word. It's being serious about what He calls serious and delighting in what He tells me to delight in.

Perhaps we should call it *balance*—a quality many of us lack, and a reason why we need each other. It is also why we need the plumb line of the Word of God to align our own tendencies and keep us from extremes.

The overly serious personality may find himself living in discord with God's Word, just as the extremely casual person does in his indifferent view toward sin. A solemn personality may not have trouble taking sin gravely, but he may not obey God when he says, "Rejoice . . . delight . . . shout for joy," or listen when He says, "don't be anxious" and "don't provoke your children to anger."

If we search God's Word and find His truth, we'll find the balance in commands such as "*strive* to enter His *rest*" and "be *strong* in the *grace* of the Lord Jesus." To me, the "strive" and the "be strong" are qualities of the serious person and the "rest" and the "grace" are strengths of the relaxed personality.

We're commanded to be both . . . which must be one reason why God often puts opposites together.

Solemn people need lighthearted companions to keep them from taking themselves—and life's circumstances—*too* seriously. They need assistance to enjoy each day; to cast their burdens on the Lord; to squeeze from the moments of each day all the happiness they contain.

But casual individuals require serious people for a great many other reasons—to learn discipline, to practice being sober and serious about the things and commands of God.

We've discussed only two facets of a serious or lighthearted approach to life. I hope you'll think of many others in the days ahead.

But first, have you identified your inclination in this area and how it affects your attitude and response toward life? Do you know what part of your approach to life is from your background? What you've learned from Scripture? Your personality?

Do these words describe you?

thoughtful	sincere
pensive	earnest
grave	determined
solemn	resolute
sedate	resolved
staid	purposeful
sober	

Obviously, if you identify with most of these, we'll name you Serious.

And if you're Casual? Try on these words:

unplanned	informal
haphazard	random
offhand	relaxed
easygoing	lackadaisical
spontaneous	unsystematic
slapdash	sporadic

I must admit, I hope you and your spouse are identifying yourselves in different columns. If you are, you will more easily attain equilibrium between grim and happy-go-lucky, harmony between serious and relaxed, parity between resolute and easy, and equanimity between resolved yet *enjoying*. You will also be filling in the cracks with the cement that binds you together as a couple.

That, my friends, is balance.

And that, I believe, is also *maturity*.

19

Lean on Me
DEPENDENT VS. INDEPENDENT

CAROLE

I fought back the tears and waved until the plane taxied from the gate. My kids and grandkids were headed home to Mexico. Were we going to miss them!

Driving the sixty miles to Denver's Stapleton Airport was a small price to pay to save the time, money, and frustration of changing planes from Colorado Springs with two small children (one in a cast for a broken arm).

As I walked back to my car parked in the farthest section of the garage, I prayed for my family. My thoughts stayed with them as I maneuvered the car through the crowded streets of Denver out onto the freeway, stopped midway along the route home at Castle Rock for gas, and then guided my car once again onto the interstate for the final leg of the trip.

I was well on my way when I noticed a faint wisp of steam coming from the front of the car. At first I was puzzled, but then dismissed it as evaporation due to the warm winter sun and sped on. But wait—was that more steam? It really did look like it. I glanced at the dash just in time to see the glaring red emergency light start flashing.

"Oh, no!" I thought and pulled hastily over to the side of the road. I was two miles out of Castle Rock with no exit or filling station ahead for many lonely miles. What should I *do*?

161

As I stopped, steam poured from the engine. Or was it smoke? I got out of the car as fast as possible and stood surveying the scene from a safe distance. Clouds of vapor filled the air but no fire that I could see.

"What now?" I thought, feeling helpless. I consoled myself with the knowledge that I did have my Triple A card with me.

As I locked the car and started across the median to walk back to Castle Rock, a car pulled off the road and stopped near me. A middle-aged man emerged and asked, "Need some help?"

Dumbly, I nodded and he suggested, "Let's open the hood and see if we can find what the problem is."

Sheepishly I asked, "How do you open the hood?"

Together we found the latch. His diagnosis (which was obvious as he pointed out the offending part) was a split radiator hose. I groaned.

He graciously offered to take me back to Castle Rock—a fourteen-mile trip for him, because the turnaround was miles ahead—and left me at a service station. From there I was directed to the AAA station.

A few minutes later I was seated in the tow truck as the driver hooked up my vehicle to his. I watched the trailing car anxiously as it was pulled like a lopsided drunk (bad suspension, I discovered) back to the station. I waited a frustrating three hours on the steps of the station until the mechanic had located the correct hose and driven some miles to get it in order to replace the damaged one. Finally, rather shakily, I headed home again.

Later, I clipped a Ziggy cartoon that described it all. Ziggy is trying to fix a chair leg that he sawed off too short and, looking woebegone, he says, "Of all the things I never was . . . being 'handy' is one of my most wasn't!!"[1]

Let's look at this incident in light of who I am. Would I have even had a Triple A card if Jack hadn't put one in my purse and carefully instructed me about how to use it? (Answer: probably not.) Do I *yet* know how to get the hood of the car up? (Answer: are you kidding?) Would I know a radiator hose from an elephant's trunk? (Hmmm, well, maybe.) Do I know how to put oil in the car? (Well, I do know you *use* oil in a car.)

I *have* learned to fill the gas tank—out of necessity, I assure you. I do drive and fly alone. I even know to ask about my frequent flyer points—but it was Jack who gave me the card with the number on it. I wish I could tell you that my feelings during this incident aren't typical. But in all honesty, I can't say that because frequently I find myself in situations where an internal button lights up that says, "Help! I need Jack!"

Most times I don't even realize how much I depend on Jack—until something like a broken radiator hose happens. Then I *think* about how much I depend on him and thank God for a husband who is a caregiver. I need care in a big way, for I tend to have a dependent nature.

Oh, you might not think so at times. At certain social functions, I probably appear at ease and in control. But if you could look inside me, you would see that mentally I'm hanging on to Jack's coattails. Even if he's clear across the room, I find security in his presence.

I identify with a song called "The Warrior Is a Child"; while I may look strong out there fighting the world, when I'm alone, I cry and need a helping hand, because in reality, the "warrior is a child."

Looking strong, but feeling weak. Appearing confident, but feeling inadequate and helpless.

All right. So I have a dependent nature. That's okay. It's the way I was born. However, don't let me confuse you, because as I see it dependence is no excuse for *helplessness*.

Times come in most of our lives when we seek to lean on someone or something only to find nothing there to rely on. Perhaps we've lost a job that afforded security, or we've been pushed out of the nest and remain single, or divorced after a painful marriage, or widowed after years of leaning on a supporting spouse. We hear stories of women who find themselves alone and lost because they've never balanced a checkbook, traveled alone, or driven a car. Many have no job skills. Having been dependent on their husbands (or parents, children, friends), they are helpless when left alone.

I ache inside for these women—but I wonder about them, too. And I question the husband who, in his caregiving days, didn't consider the possibility that his wife would need to know how to take care of herself one day.

Jack has a book in his library called *How to Train Your Wife to Be a Widow*. He bought and read it out of love for me. And he's been faithful to practice it, too! He has kept me abreast of our complete financial picture, encouraged me to venture out into the world by myself, provided me with needed skills (though I still have trouble balancing the checkbook!). No, I couldn't complete our income tax return—but I know who can do it for me. I know the people at the garage who repair my Honda; I've got the plumber's name in my address pages; and I have some working skills if needed. For much of the above, I have Jack to thank.

So if you are married to a dependent person, your challenge is to help that one learn to grow in competence. If you *are* that person, then by God's grace, determine what it will take to become able to cope with life by yourself. Not without God, of course. But, should it become necessary, without a spouse.

I am by nature dependent, but Jack was born independent—and I'm glad. Not that independent people will always feel secure and capable and will never have times of fear and inadequacy, but they will fight those feelings and work at not experiencing them for long. They will take charge of the situation, make advanced preparation in case it happens again, and fight to be in control next time.

Listen to the synonyms for "independent": self-reliant, uncontrolled, on one's own, autonomous, free, self-directing, individualistic, uncoerced, unconstrained, free from the control or influence of others.

Now look at the antonyms: dependent, influenced, controlled, directed, subordinate, subject, servile, attached, interrelated. ("Slavish" can be one too!)

A person who has an independent nature will cope—with life, job, disappointment, relationships, circumstances. That's one of the good parts.

But independence can become detachment or total autonomy. It may become a nature without checks and balances, perhaps one that resists being dependent even upon God Himself who says we are to depend upon Him and realize our need for one another. "The eye cannot say to the hand, 'I don't need you!' And the head cannot say to the feet, 'I don't need you!' On the contrary, those parts of the body that seem to be weaker are indispensable" (1 Corinthians 12:21-22).

In marriage, independence can destroy a relationship just as surely as an overly-dependent personality.

The Independent Husband

Everyone has the yearning way down deep to be needed. If I felt Jack didn't need me for *anything*, I'd feel less of a person, cut off, pushed away. I *need* Jack to need me. And he does. As capable and independent as he is, I am essential to him. He tells me that often. In fact, I think he *looks* for ways to need me (and I love him for that).

Oh, of course he's needed me as the mother of Lynn and to be the hostess, the cook, the housekeeper. But what an encouragement it is when he tells me that he finds me indispensable as his sounding board, his counselor, and most of all his companion. In realizing that I need to be needed, he has shown me the deepest kind of love.

The Independent Wife

If it's the wife who has all the makings of an independent nature, there are particular consequences that may result. Scripture has much to say about the attitude of a wife toward her husband. The Amplified version of the Bible—which takes the Greek word of the New Testament and gives it all the rich meanings of the original language—renders Ephesians 5:33, "Let the wife see that she respects and reverences her husband—that she notices him, regards him, honors him, prefers him, venerates and esteems him; and that she defers to him, praises him, and loves and admires him exceedingly."

When I read that list, I think, "Wow! That's *all* I have to do? That will take the rest of my life!"

Independence doesn't jell too well with that list, does it? But wives, let me tell you something. *God never gives a command that He will not enable you to do.* If you have been born with an independent nature, praise God. It means He has a special job for you to do that needs that personality. But it no doubt also means that you will need extra grace to allow Him to blend and soften that independence to the place where you can practice being the kind of godly wife He commands you to be. Hang onto His wonderful promise in 2 Corinthians 12:9 where Christ says, "My grace is sufficient for you." I think of grace as "anything you need whenever you need it." That's not very theological-sounding but it's true.

Even though I'm dependent by nature, I also have a stubborn, *independent* streak running right up my backbone, which sticks out like porcupine quills at the oddest, awfullest moments, and with poisoned barbs pokes painfully into another's ego. I've struggled with it, been defeated, and finally prayed for God's grace. It still erupts now and then, and God and I are even yet working to blunt those sharp projections. I trust it is happening.

Jack and I pray for balance and stability. We need to be dependent on God—and on others in a healthy way. We also need independence in order to be strong, courageous, and resourceful. Furthermore, as a couple, Jack and I need interdependence so that we two *are* really becoming one.

Is that your desire and prayer? If so, God will enable you.

Who knows, maybe I'll even learn how to put oil in my car!

NOTE:
1. Tom Wilson, "Ziggy," September 19, 1977.

20

Who Wrote the Script?
THE INFLUENCE OF BACKGROUNDS

JACK

Scripts. That's the difficulty.

"When two actors go out on stage, we take it for granted that they both are going to be working from the same script," said Dr. Carlfred Broderick. "By the same token, when two people marry they put down their five dollars in a similar hope that they can take a particular script for granted. Unfortunately, the scripts from which each member of a couple plays her and his marital scenes are sometimes very different. . . . Often our scripts are based on our parents' marriages."[1]

Some people say that we each have distinctly different "tapes" playing in our heads that dictate our actions. But I like the idea of "scripts," don't you?

Dr. Broderick tells of a man from a family of five with strict rules for sharing their two bathrooms. When the door was shut, no one would think even of knocking, let alone entering.

This young man married a woman from a family of five people with only one bathroom, and everyone had walked in and out of that one bathroom at will. So of course she never gave a thought to walking in on her husband in *their* bathroom. He, however, was so taken aback that he couldn't speak![2]

Then Dr. Broderick gives an example from his own marriage:

In the early days of my own marriage I would have sworn that my wife and I had discussed every aspect of life and love. We had known each other from kindergarten, dated from the tenth grade and been engaged for a year and a half. But we never discussed what happens when you are sick. And if someone had suggested we discuss it, I would have laughed.

Every right-thinking person knows what you should do when you get sick—you go to bed. That is your part. Then your mother, or whoever loves you, pumps you full of fruit juice.

Well I married this woman I had known all my life, and in the natural course of events I caught the flu. I knew what to do, of course. I went to bed and waited. But nothing happened. Nothing. I couldn't believe it!

I was so hurt, I would have left if I hadn't been so ill. Finally I *asked* about juice and she brought me some—in a little four-ounce glass. Period. Because as I learned later, the only time they drank juice at her house was on alternate Tuesdays, when they graced breakfast with a drop in a thimble-sized glass. My family's "juice glasses" held 12 ounces and there was always someone standing by to refill them.[3]

The number of script-differences in marriage is awesome. Author Elisabeth Elliot gives us an example in her book *Discipline, the Glad Surrender* when she writes:

A couple I know had been married only a week or two when the wife went out shopping. The husband wondered what he might do for her while she was gone that would please and surprise her and show her how much he loved her. A brilliant plan came to mind. He got down on hands and knees and scrubbed the kitchen floor. It was a demeaning task in his opinion, and he felt exceedingly humble while performing it. How amazed Ann would be! He waited in eager anticipation of her return, thinking how blessed it is to give.

She drove in the driveway, breezed into the kitchen, set the grocery bags on the counter, and glanced at the floor.

"Oh—the floor's clean. Thank you, honey!" was all she said and went about putting things away.

The man told me he went into a three-day funk. He was hurt; he was insulted; he was not properly appreciated; and the blessing of giving drained out in an instant because he had not received the kind of thanks he had expected.

Ann had no idea what the trouble was. What *she* did not know was that her husband had never heard of a man's doing such a thing as scrubbing a floor for his wife, especially voluntarily, having thought of it all by himself. What *he* did not know was that in his wife's family, no woman ever did the job. Her father considered it a man's job and did it as a matter of course.[4]

Carole and I came to marriage thinking we really were approaching this drama from the same script. After all, both of us were raised in Christian homes and in middle-class neighborhoods; our parents had good marriages, loved their children, were firm but not strict disciplinarians; we attended the same college, had some of the same friends, and had gone together for three and a half years when we walked down the aisle.

So it came with some surprise when we realized that not only were we reading from unrelated scripts, but at times we didn't even seem to be on the same stage.

We ran into the two-stage problem our very first Christmas. Carole wanted to wait until Christmas morning to open gifts! Can you believe that? Every sane person knows that Christmas Eve is the time to gather around the tree and open gifts. But no. Christmas Eve, said Carole, was the time to have the Christmas story and sing carols. And then early Christmas morning, one woke in excited anticipation of stockings filled with goodies. After a hurried breakfast, the gifts would be opened one by one with each taking a turn giving out a gift to another. It took her family hours, and Christmas dinner was forgotten in the process. Imagine that! No traditional Christmas dinner.

And Christmas wasn't the only holiday we celebrated in divergent ways. There was Valentine's Day (she celebrated it, I didn't); Easter (a new outfit was essential but she had to wear it Palm Sunday so she wouldn't think about the new clothes on Easter; I can never remember having a new outfit); and the Fourth of July (big family reunion for Carole, fireworks in the park for me).

But at least you could say our stages were in the same theater.

Some aren't even in the same town. Steve and Annie Chapman in *Married Lovers, Married Friends* provide an example of this:

> While I love everything about Christmas, Steve loathes everything about it except the birth of our Savior. And even that he celebrates with reservation, since he's quick to point out that December 25 wasn't actually the Lord's birthday, and he'll tell you how the choice of that date has pagan connotations.
>
> So what happens to the glory of a smooth-working Christian marriage when the wife is Santa's helper, and the husband says, "No elves or reindeer allowed"?
>
> Our first attempt at a solution was to *compromise* in an attempt to keep peace. Steve tried to avoid a row by letting me decorate a tree. That, I grudgingly agreed, was a real compromise, since he believed the whole idea of trees and ornaments was a pagan custom that shouldn't be part of a believer's Christmas. And he allowed me to buy gifts for the children— another tough compromise since he thought all this gift-giving simply taught them materialism and greed.
>
> I tried to inject the season with what celebrating I could without offending him—and felt sorry for myself the whole time. Okay, so we had a tree, but it never would have made it at the Lennon Sisters' house. It was a dreadful aluminum thing that I picked up at a garage sale. (The box was marked $1.00, but the lady didn't put up any resistance when I offered less. So you have an idea how charming this tree really was.) And to decorate it, I baked sugar cookies with paper-clip hangers in the end, because I figured buying ornaments would send my husband into a tailspin. The kids did get gifts, but, at Steve's insistence, only one apiece.[5]

It took many years for Steve and Annie to work through this one! Annie finally gave up, deciding that her marriage was worth more than one day in the year, and unity and love were needed to be an example of Christ and His Church. Simultaneously, God worked in Steve's heart concerning the fact that he might be wounding his wife's spirit. He didn't tell Annie, though, that he'd had a change of heart until the next Christmas. In a surprise move, he took the kids and went out and bought a *live* Christmas tree complete with decorations, lights, and a tape of Christmas carols. The children continue to get only one gift, but there is joy in that home at Christmas.

Over the years Carole and I have grown together, too. We now celebrate Christmas both on Christmas Eve, with the Christmas story and carols and half our gifts—given slowly one by one—and on Christmas morning, with the rest of our gifts and a traditional Christmas dinner to boot. We've joined our traditions to make a year rich with celebrations.

But in reality, how special days are celebrated is one of the easy ones.

Scripts are especially difficult to handle in the area of ethnic differences.

We have friends who, four years into their marriage, knew they had a giant problem. She was a reserved German, he a volatile Italian. Whenever they disagreed, he raised his voice and shouted. She withdrew.

It seemed to her that he was always shouting whether they were disagreeing or not. And she withdrew even further.

Four years into their marriage, they realized she had suppressed both her feelings and her thinking to the extent that serious problems had developed in their marriage.

When they went to a counselor, he suggested that they take ten minutes to talk before the children were up. He gave them specific instructions on how to spend those ten minutes. She could talk on any topic she wished to *and he was not to say a word*. The next morning he could answer her. This gave him twenty-four hours to think about his response and be more controlled in his tone of voice. Then he could introduce another subject or add to the one she had initiated. She could not respond until the third morning.

It took them several months to work through the backlog of things she'd been repressing, but today they have one of the most beautiful marriages you'd want to see.

But more important than whether the differences are from varying ethnic backgrounds is the need to recognize that those differences do exist. I recently read this example:

Martha Stein grew up in a home where discretion and privacy were prized. Her husband, David, was raised in a family in which everyone knew—and felt he had a right to know—everyone else's business.

"I was enchanted by David's family," Martha says. "The first time he took me home for dinner, every member gave a full report on his day. There were comments and laughter about everything from his sister's new dress to David's new boss. In my family, 'Please pass the peas' was the extent of dinner conversation."

Martha was upset, however, when David told his parents—on the very day he and Martha agreed to stop using birth control—that they were trying to have a baby. "I just couldn't believe it," she remembers. "There he was, discussing the most intimate details of our life with other people. When I told him how I felt, he said, 'But they're not other people; they're my family.'"

In their own relationship, David sometimes felt that Martha was "closed off" and unwilling to share her deepest feelings with him.

"We often argued because we thought these differences were deliberate attempts to drive the other crazy," Martha says. "In time, we came to see that our conflicts had nothing to do with a lack of love for each other, but with the very different styles of the families in which we were raised."[6]

If your family rarely sat down for a meal together, you'll have trouble making the evening meal a priority for companionship.

Author Lavonne Neff says at the time of her marriage, her parents had been married for thirty-five years and her husband's for twenty-five. Both marriages were solid. But, she says, "We had instinctively learned patterns of behavior that had worked well for our parents, and we didn't think twice about applying them to ourselves.

"And that was the problem—David was treating me just as his father treats his mother, and I was responding just as my mother responds to my father.

"The trouble was that his father was not married to my mother!"[7]

If you took a video of marriages around the world, many pictures would emerge.

You would see some in which the husband fathers both wife and children. There would be others in which the wife supports the family and dominates and controls both husband and children. In a few cultures, the picture might emerge of a husband with several wives who are responsible not only to him, but also to his relatives.

God's plan for the family is an equilateral triangle with God at the top. At the base are equal partners who are best friends, committed to God and to each other. This is the kind of marriage in which trust, friendship, commitment, joy, and union thrive.

If you are engaged to be married, or even if you've been married a few years ("few" is relative!), ask some questions of yourself and your spouse to avoid misunderstandings in the future or solve them in the present. We suggest the two of you take an hour or two for several weeks and explore the following:

1. What were the responsibilities and chores of each member of your family as you were growing up? How were these accepted by each member? (For example, did they accept them as routine, resent them, gripe about them, try to get out of them?)

2. In your opinion, how should chores for the home, car, lawn, garden, etc., be handled? Who should decide who does what?

3. What holidays did your family celebrate and how? What, of their traditions, do you want to continue in our family? Do you want to add any? How important is this to you? Was Christmas of special importance in your home? How much was spent on gifts?

4. Were table manners and manners in general taught in your home? How diligently? What manners are most important to you? (For example, is chewing with one's mouth closed important? Using a knife and fork properly? Opening doors for women? Being helped on with your coat? Not interrupting someone who's speaking?)

5. What was your parents' educational background? Was good English used in your home? How important is the proper use of grammar to you? Is this something you want our family to work on?

6. In what events did your family participate together? Which meals did you eat together as a family? What recreation did you all participate in? Work projects? Did you worship together? Have family devotions? Other? What did you like about this? Dislike? What would you like our family to do together regularly?

7. What was the general atmosphere around your home? Was there much quarreling or was it mostly pleasant? Which member of your

family did you enjoy being with the most? The least?

8. How important in your home were reunions and get-togethers with relatives? How important is your extended family to you? How often would you like to see them?

9. How did your family spend vacations? If your family had $200 to spend on a vacation but the house needed painting, would your father have wanted to use that money to paint the house during vacation or go somewhere inexpensive? What about your mother? What would you want to do? What is your ideal vacation, given unlimited funds? Given very limited funds?

10. What was each member of your family's attitude about God? About church? About spiritual things in general? Which ones were Christians? Which ones were hostile about spiritual matters? Did you go to church regularly as a family? How committed was your family to that? What is your own feeling concerning God, Christ, the Christian life? How do you feel about regular church attendance and what does "regular" mean to you? What were your families' views concerning Sunday as the Lord's Day?

11. What value was held in highest esteem by your father (for example, honesty, integrity, faithfulness, love, kindness)? Your mother? What other values were important and how was that demonstrated? What values are most important to you and how would you like to see them worked out in our home?

12. What was the pattern of your family's social life (country club, sports events, big parties, small dinners, games, etc.)? What would you like to continue that you enjoyed? What kinds of things do you dislike?

13. To what extent did your father and mother show an interest in what you were doing? Did they get involved in school activities? Come to events in which you were participating? See that you had your homework done?

14. What were the rules of conduct in your home? Did you have strict deadlines when you had to be home in the evenings? Rules about dating? Did your parents insist on knowing where you were most of the time? Did each member of the family keep the others informed of their whereabouts?

15. What was the attitude of your family concerning privacy? Did you walk in and out of bedrooms and bathrooms without knocking?

What would you like to do in your home concerning this?

16. Was your family conservative or liberal in their thinking? About politics? Religion? What were your families' views on: Abortion? Alcohol? Cigarettes? Drugs? Racial issues?

17. Did your parents teach you about sex? At what age? Was their view of sex healthy? Would you want your children to be raised as you were in this regard? If you didn't learn about sex from your parents, where and what did you learn about it?

18. What kinds of attitudes did your father and mother have concerning money? Were they liberal spenders? Givers? Savers? Did your family operate on a budget? Were they in debt much of the time? If so, from whom did they borrow? Would they be more likely to spend money on new cars, clothes, entertainment, insurance, or other? What were their priorities as far as money was concerned? Which of their values would you want to emulate? What would you want to avoid?

19. How well do you feel your parents related to one another? To each member of the family? What would you like to carry over from them or avoid?

20. What did your family read? What programs did they watch on television? What kind of movies did they enjoy?

21. What kinds of humor did your family enjoy? (Practical jokes? Puns? Slapstick?)

22. What kinds of pets did your family own? Were they treated as members of the family or kept outside? How do you feel about animals?

23. Did an older relative ever live with your family? What was your parents' attitude toward the widowed or sick and their responsibility toward them?

24. How did your family respond to illness (with sympathy, over-concern, ignored it and went on working, etc.)? When you were ill, how did your family treat you? How would you like to be treated?

I realize that's quite a list. And it isn't even comprehensive. But it is a *beginning* of rewriting part of your script in order to approach the drama of marriage with understanding.

Someone has said, "A successful marriage requires falling in love many times, always with the same person."[8]

That's true. Part of the process of falling in love—and *staying* in love—demands a knowledge and understanding of the background of our partner. This awareness comes through hard work, communication, compromise, adjusting.

And a giant helping of God's grace.

NOTES:
1. Carlfred Broderick, "How to Rewrite Your Marriage Script So It Works," *Redbook* (February 1979), page 21.
2. Broderick, page 21.
3. Susan Jacoby, "When Opposites Attract," *Readers Digest* (December 1986), page 95.
4. Elisabeth Elliot, *Discipline, the Glad Surrender* (Old Tappan, NJ: Fleming H. Revell, 1982).
5. Steve and Annie Chapman, *Married Lovers, Married Friends* (Minneapolis: Bethany House Publishers, 1989), page 45.
6. LaVonne Neff, "The Marriage You Grew Up With," *Partnership* (September-October 1987), page 28.
7. Neff, page 28.
8. Mignon McLaughlin in *The Atlantic*, quoted in "Quotable Quotes," *Readers Digest* (July 1989), page 8.

21
Let's Talk About the Weather

THE CLIMATE OF PRAISE

CAROLE

When we lived in California, someone told me that the first year there, you were a critic. The second year you became a booster. And the third year you developed into a downright liar!

The very day we moved to Colorado, I found myself skipping the "year of the critic" and at *least* jumped into the booster category. The Colorado Springs Tourist Bureau ought to put me on its payroll.

Now I must admit that yesterday one of our occasional summer hailstorms stripped most of the leaves off my geraniums. And we are frequently bombarded by wild thunder and lightning storms. Snow blankets our city unseasonably several times each year, sometimes as early as September and as late as June. (Freaky!)

But let me tell you, the overall climate in Colorado Springs is *great!* Most mornings are sunny, moderate, and beautiful. It's a dry climate, so hot days don't seem so hot and cold days seem less cold. We love it.

If the marriage climate is upbeat, positive, and loving, it can endure some thundershowers, hail, and even unseasonable snow. But if the overall climate is dark and gloomy, the occasional storms may be unendurable.

Marriages can tolerate a number of differences between two people, even if they aren't worked through to becoming possibilities instead of problems, *if the climate is good.*

177

In our world today, the overall climate for marriage is gloom and doom. Pessimism abounds. Bruce Shelley says, "Many people think the marriage match is fixed. The chances for a happy, successful marriage are none too good at best. They are almost impossible if we do nothing to prepare ourselves or our children for it." He goes on to say that "Married life is a lot of different things to different people. French historian Hippolyte Taine said that marriage could be summed up as 'three weeks of curiosity, three months of love, and thirty years of tolerance.'"[1]

Isn't that sad? To think that what people expect is to "tolerate," is intolerable—for we must *love*, and love deeply. That takes working at it. It takes commitment—the kind of commitment that refuses to entertain the idea of divorce if things don't work out the way we'd hoped. The kind of commitment and determination that will work *through* no matter the cost.

It also takes refusing to be negative both about marriage and about the one I'm "one" with. In the midst of a world that conveys negative messages about marriage, that isn't easy.

These negative views are stated and restated all around us—in humor, for example.

In a cartoon, a man at a bar is saying to his buddy, "Marriage has been good for me, Herbie. Suffering builds character."[2]

A woman offers an episode from her married life as a humorous anecdote:

> After ten years of widowhood, I remarried. Leaving work one wintry evening, I told a colleague that it was very gratifying to once again have someone worry about me if the roads were icy. My new husband would be awaiting my arrival, I said, and would hurry out to meet me at the car.
> I couldn't have been more right. As I pulled into the driveway, my husband burst out the door and came up to me. Rubbing our new car, he anxiously queried, "Did you get salt on it?"[3]

Somehow I don't find these too funny. They contribute to a negative climate.

Listen to these remarks, each of them from a couple who loves each other:

Husband (jokingly), "My wife, Sue, had other plans, so I made arrangements to take this cute little blonde to the banquet—but then Sue changed her plans and I ended up having to take my wife!" (said with pretended disgust).

Wife to husband as she was talking to a friend, "Would you please go to bed—we're in the middle of discussing something *important*."

Wife to husband after discussing plans to go out to dinner with her husband and a woman friend of hers, "You won't be home until 6:45? Well, don't hurry then. We'll go on without you and you can grab some fast food on your way home."

I'm not making these up. And the sad part is, these people weren't even *aware* of their putdowns. The last one wasn't overtly a putdown, but it graphically showed the husband his wife's preference of a dinner companion. His company wasn't worth waiting for.

The jokes abound:

■ He brags that he's the boss in his home, but he lies about other things, too.

■ When she wants his opinion, she gives it to him.

■ She snaps, "Are you a man or a mouse?—squeak up."

■ The last big decision she let him make was whether to wash or dry.

You get the picture.

Do you see any of your attitudes in it? What is the general climate of your marriage? Would you say that the atmosphere in your home is warm, positive, and encouraging—or cool, critical, and discouraging?

One of the most important ingredients for a good climate—one of the most vital ways to deepen love—is *praise*.

It has been suggested that love grows in primarily two ways: first by doing enjoyable things together; second, by reinforcing behavior in the other that you appreciate. I'd love to see more positive examples in books, magazines, and television of these ways to develop love. Very occasionally, I find one:

Last year my wife and I toured New England by car. One afternoon we stopped at a farmhouse that sold fresh apple cider. An elderly farmer and his wife greeted us.

As we sipped cider, the old man remarked that he and his wife had been happily married for nearly fifty years. Then he added, "I reckon the best marriages are really mutual-admiration societies. Elsie likes a little compliment from time to time—and so do I."

This bit of rural philosophy brought to mind Oliver Wendell Holmes's description of friendship as "the pleasing game of interchanging praise." Yet how many spouses praise each other for maneuvering the car through difficult traffic? And how many husbands praise their wives for remembering to sew on a shirt button?

Praise brings warmth and pleasure into the commonplace and turns the noisy rattle of the world into music.[4]

The author goes on to say we should make a point to praise something at least once a day—for "praise is like sunlight to the human spirit; we cannot flower and grow without it."[5]

God has much to say about praise: "Pleasant words are a honeycomb, sweet to the soul and healing to the bones" (Proverbs 16:24).

+ + +

Most books on love, marriage, and friendship have a chapter on building up the ego of the one you love. You read how a wife is to encourage her husband with such things as taking the pressure off when he's under stress by smoothing the way for him; by not making big issues of small matters; by postponing decisions that may involve arguments until the crisis is past; and by dealing with the normal daily problems of children and house quietly by herself. She needs to learn how to accentuate the positive; not take him for granted; attack the deed, not the man; and above all *listen*.

One writer puts it this way, "The woman who is able to heal her husband's wounds, to make him feel that to *her*, anyway, he is the most important person in the world, will earn from him an undying gratitude that will pay her infinite dividends the rest of her married life."[6]

You've heard it all before. You may even have made up lists of things to *do*—such as "Give several hugs every day." And I'm not against lists. In fact, I hope you have one and pick up ideas from every source available. But my question remains: Have you created the *climate*? To create a climate, you must realize that praise itself is first of all an *attitude*—an attitude about our spouse that in turn affects our entire outlook.

The heartbeat of the home in which I grew up throbbed with love and encouragement—a climate brought about mainly by my mother. It wasn't until years later that I realized it was her *attitude* that created this climate. I asked her once why she had never complained in the midst of circumstances I knew must have been difficult for her: "Why Carole," she exclaimed, "I was with your *father*!"

Mom had created such a climate of praise and appreciation within her marriage that it affected her whole view of life.

If the climate is there, the compliment-sunbeams and praise-lights that nurture a person's ego will shine naturally. They'll sparkle in private and glitter in public—which is also crucial. For praise must not be limited to behind the doors of our homes. It must be heralded for the world to hear. "One characteristic above all others distinguishes marriages that last: the willingness of husband and wife to testify in public in each other's behalf. If a husband or wife occasionally offers public praise indicating downright pride in his or her mate, nothing really bad should happen to their union."[7]

Private praise. Public accolades. And continuous signs of affection. These make up the warm and sunny climate in which love thrives and grows.

Perhaps you may be thinking that you are a serious, calm, independent personality. Expressions of praise, encouragement, or compliments don't come easily for you.

Sorry. No excuses accepted.

Why? To be obedient to God, we are to build up and encourage one another. And God not only will teach us *how*, but has given us His Holy Spirit to help us do it—that One of whom He says, "But the fruit of the Spirit is love, joy, peace, patience, kindness, goodness, faithfulness, gentleness and self-control" (Galatians 5:22-23).

If we are not measuring up well against *that* standard, perhaps we are not listening closely enough to God, who continues to whisper to us, "Grow in *grace* and in the knowledge of the Lord Jesus Christ."

NOTES:
1. Bruce Shelley, "Danger Signs in Marriage," *The Christian Reader* (March 1967), page 21.
2. Bill Hoest, "The Lockhorns."
3. L. Catherine Ferguson, "Life In These United States," *Readers Digest* (December 1986), page 94.
4. Henry N. Ferguson, "Take Out Some Marriage Insurance," *Readers Digest* (May 1987), page 213.
5. Ferguson, page 214.
6. James Lincoln Collier, "How To Support Your Husband's Ego," *Readers Digest* (January 1970), page 108.
7. Collier, page 108.

PART V

THE WAY WE
LOOK AT LIFE

22

Is the Glass Half Empty or Half Full?

PESSIMISTIC VS. OPTIMISTIC

JACK

A giant sun is setting behind Ziggy, a dyed-in-the-wool pessimist. He sits in a dark shadow with his head in his hands saying, "I believe in living life one doldrum at a time."[1] Ziggy does not live in the sunshine.

Contrast the optimist—"the kind of person who believes a housefly is looking for a way out."[2]

I recently picked up an article by the actor Kirk Douglas and grinned ruefully. He said of his wife and himself, "We have very different temperaments. Once I said to her, 'You're always happy unless something comes along to make you unhappy. I'm always unhappy unless something comes along to make me happy. And even then I'm not sure I'm happy.'"[3]

The old saying goes, "The pessimist sees the difficulty in every opportunity, and the optimist sees the opportunity in every difficulty."[4]

Webster defines optimism as the doctrine that the existing world is the best possible; that good ultimately prevails over evil. It is the tendency to take the most hopeful or cheerful view of matters or to expect the best outcome. It is the practice of looking on the bright side of things.

Pessimism is the doctrine or belief that the existing world is the worst possible; that evil in life outweighs the good. It is the tendency to expect misfortune or the worst outcome in any circumstances. It is the practice of looking on the dark side of things.

Most pessimists wouldn't agree with that definition. They would instead consider themselves *realists*. Their view of optimists would differ, too. Optimists, to them, tend to have a "Pollyanna" outlook; they don't approach things in a down-to-earth manner.

We need to know our own general tendencies and all our exceptions as well as those of our partner.

If we use *Webster*'s definitions, Carole and I combine the traits of optimism and pessimism. We'd both say that the existing world isn't all that great but that good (God) will ultimately prevail over evil (Satan). But the rest of Webster's definition would find us going separate ways. We vary in taking the most hopeful or cheerful view of matters or expecting the best outcome. Our expectations of misfortune or "worst outcome" depend on the day and the subject matter.

You would guess that Carole, being the extroverted, part-sanguine personality that she is, would be the embodiment of optimism, and that I, being the introverted, more serious one, would be the essence of pessimism. But it isn't quite that simple. Because of her imagination, her propensity for the "what if's" and for projecting the future, many times Carole is the one to worry about negative outcomes. She'll say, "We're too late—we probably won't get a flight." And I'll say, "Oh, we'll get one" (and generally we do).

She'll say, "What if no one's there to meet us?" and I'll say, "It'll be okay."

I plan for the future, too, and try to anticipate possible problems—financially, for instance. But while I *plan* for them, I don't *dwell* on them. I live in the present even while making future preparations.

Carole gets up each day wondering what lies ahead. I get up each day.

Carole gets on airplanes with anticipation—or anxiety. I get on airplanes.

Carole's mind races with possibilities. My mind concentrates on solving problems.

But when Carole gets *down*, she scrapes bottom. We're talking *gloom*. Fortunately, it doesn't usually last very long—a few hours, at most a day or two, and then she's on top once again.

I guess I'd have to say that Carole has an "up" nature, but because of her active imagination to project things that haven't happened, she has to battle "down" thinking.

I have a line personality, not particularly up or down. I tend to look at politics, trends, what's happening in our world pessimistically (I want to say *realistically*). But ask me if my grandson is going to be a dynamo for the Lord, an outstanding leader, or a great golfer some day—man, I'm the greatest optimist! Ask me if my granddaughter is going to be a woman of God, lovely to look at, and fabulous to know—I'll say *of course*. Ask me if Carole and I are going to grow old with health and joy—I'll say, you bet!

Most people are not any more consistent in their approach to the area of optimism and pessimism than we are. However, the need is to study yourself and your mate in order to know the way you are *generally* and then the way you are in given situations.

We should *always be learning*.

Several years ago, Carole and I were returning from a trip to Florida in January after two weeks of intense ministry. We found ourselves in the Dallas-Fort Worth airport in the middle of one of the worst ice and snow storms they had had in years. It was four degrees above zero and the unusual cold wreaked havoc at the airport. The trams weren't running, the terminal was freezing, the electric clocks were spinning wildly. We were dead tired and our heads were hurting as we waited in the cold for a bus to transfer us from one terminal to another.

I was standing there with my hands in my pockets, head down, silent.

Carole was standing next to me, and next to her was a little old lady who was extremely worried about whether she was going to make her next flight. Carole started encouraging her: "Don't worry about it . . . all the planes are running late . . . you'll make it in plenty of time . . ." and on and on. Yak. Yak. Yak.

In a few moments, her talking began to intrude on my thinking. I took my hand out of my pocket, doubled up my fist, and nudged her on the thigh. In nonverbal language, I was saying, "Shut up."

She got the message. (She hardly said two words the rest of the way home!)

In a matter of seconds, I realized I had made a giant mistake. So as we got on the bus, I put my arm around her and said, "Honey, I'm sorry. I wasn't thinking about you. Please forgive me." She grunted noncommittally.

When we got on the flight home, I apologized again—maybe two or three times—and when we arrived home at 2:00 a.m., we both apologized and went to bed with peace between us. We have made it a practice not to let the sun go down on our anger (Ephesians 4:26), but I have to admit, sometimes that sun sets *very* late in our household!

We find that most couples are content to let it end right there. The last thing they want to do is bring the subject up again and risk another blow-up and apology. It's over! They mentally sigh with relief.

But if we do that we have passed up one of life's richest opportunities to learn about each other and about ourselves.

So the next morning, after a good night's rest, verbally we went back to the Dallas airport and discussed at length what really happened.

As we explored our feelings of the night before and our responses to those feelings, we discovered something about ourselves that we hadn't known before.

We had both been feeling just about the same—achy, tired, frustrated, cold. But our reactions were totally different.

As we talked, we realized that Carole's reaction to a frustrating situation is *forced cheerfulness*. When she isn't feeling good, she forces herself to be cheerful. One way she does this is to find someone else to cheer up—in this case, the little old lady.

On the other hand, I respond by withdrawing—head down, hands in pockets. Why? Well, basically I'm a problem solver. (My daughter has told me more than once: "Dad, if you didn't have a problem to solve, you'd find one." No doubt she's right.) So at the airport in Dallas that evening, I was having an imaginary conversation with the airport manager and *we* were solving this problem that *we* had of how to get the planes running on time, the clocks repaired, the heat on. And when I'm deep into solving a problem, I don't like to be disturbed!

Now we didn't discover this in five minutes. We had to pray for God's wisdom to know it ourselves, to be vulnerable enough to each other to talk about it fully. We had to *work* at knowing ourselves and then at understanding the other. We talked for probably two hours before figuring it out.

Then Carole asked the loaded question: "Well, next time I will really try not to be so talkative in a situation like last night. But if I *can't*, what should I do?"

Gentlemen, think long and hard when you're asked a question like that one! I finally answered, truthfully, "Honey, I want you to be yourself."

Sure enough, about three months later we found ourselves in a similar situation. There I was—head down, hands in pockets, thinking. And there was Carole—and next to her was a twelve-year-old boy who was lost! And she started encouraging him . . . and encouraging him . . . and encouraging him. Finally her talking began to penetrate my concentration. But instead of getting irritated, I smiled to myself and mentally said, "Sic 'em, honey. Go to it!"

Because *now I understood.*

Sometimes Carole's determination to be cheerful in difficult situations makes her appear to be the optimist. That in itself isn't significant. The important thing is for both partners to understand the reactions of the other and give them the gift of acceptance. Life itself gives us many opportunities to understand, to share, to laugh together at frustrating situations . . . and, if we will, to learn.

It is imperative that we *look to the Word of God* to find the balance.

Does everything look black to you? Like Kirk Douglas, does it take an external trigger to make you happy—and even then you're not sure you're happy? Or are you afraid to face the dark side? Perhaps you refuse to look squarely at unpleasant or repulsive situations, and you are adamant in your refusal to drink fully of the cup of sorrow that God has allowed in your life.

Although we are created with distinct personalities and tendencies concerning our outlook on life, we do not have to be extreme—nor *should* we be. God says we are to be serious, sober, strong, wise. But we are also to delight, laugh, be full of hope and *rejoice*. He commands it again and again. "Rejoice in the Lord always. I will say it again: Rejoice!" (Philippians 4:4).

We can, with David, encourage ourselves in the Lord. But at other times, God uses our spouses to encourage and help us.

"One of the highest of human duties is the duty of encouragement," says William Barclay. "It is easy to laugh at men's ideals: it is easy to pour cold water on their enthusiasm; it is easy to discourage others. The world is full of discouragers. We have a Christian duty to encourage one another. Many a time a word of praise or thanks or appreciation or cheer has kept a man on his feet. Blessed is the man who speaks such a word."[5]

Carole recently wrote the following after attending a conference in Nebraska:

> The first thing I saw was her radiant smile as she sat in the audience. It sparkled. It encouraged.
>
> The second thing I noticed about her was the wheelchair.
>
> The third thing was that she didn't have any legs.
>
> I approached her after the meeting and as we chatted, I discovered that her situation was fairly recent. A diabetic, she had cut her toenails too close, infection and gangrene had followed, and both her legs were lost. Her vision was failing as well.
>
> But her smile! Nothing had erased that smile.
>
> I commented on that. I said, "It must be very difficult to smile when you have been through such pain."
>
> Her soft reply was, "Oh, but *God* hasn't changed."
>
> All weekend that woman's smile blessed and encouraged me right down to the soles of my soul.

Whether you are by nature an optimist or the most dour pessimist, God commands both seriousness and joyfulness *at the same time*. We are to be serious about those things He calls serious and cheerful—full of joy—in our attitude toward life *simultaneously*. To be an encourager is not optional. To be "sober" is a necessity.

To one degree or another, *all* are required by *all* of us. This is balance—a balance that means:

. . . being real in our optimism and cheerful in our pessimism.

. . . looking life in the eye and still *rejoicing*!

Will you do it?

NOTES:
1. Tom Wilson, "Ziggy," April 7, 1987.
2. George Jean Nathan in "Quotable Quotes," *Readers Digest* (April 1989), page 21.

3. Kirk Douglas, "Life's Been Good to Me," *Good Housekeeping* (August 1988), page 173.
4. Roger Ailes with Jon Kraushar, "Secrets of Successful Leaders," *Readers Digest* (May 1988), page 134.
5. William Barclay, "The Letter to the Hebrews," *The Daily Study Bible* (Edinburgh: The St. Andrew Press, 1955), pages 137-138.

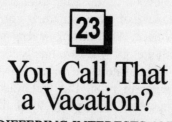

You Call That a Vacation?

DIFFERING INTERESTS AND SOCIAL STYLES

CAROLE

Vacations are revealing.

They say (whoever *they* are) that many couples decide to divorce following a vacation together.

I think I can understand that. After all, a couple is together unremittingly sixty seconds of sixty minutes of twenty-four hours of each and every day on a vacation. Even the best of friendships may not survive intact in that framework.

But recently, we identified another kind of meatball in the spaghetti sauce.

Vacations offer an otherwise unafforded opportunity for differences—especially contrasts in *interests*—to come to the surface, which in the rush and schedules of everyday living might never be so blatantly revealed.

A trip to England not too long ago left me wondering.

In researching the trip, Jack came upon an article that mentioned a book about a couple of off-the-beaten-track golf courses. Jack thought the book might be worth looking at, but it proved unavailable in the U.S.

Thus began Our Search.

We had a few days to meander around the quaint towns of Devon and soon established a pattern. At our hotel or bed-and-breakfast place, we'd look in the phonebook for the address of a local bookstore. Then we would brave the maze of winding streets and hunt patiently for a hard-to-find parking place. After asking several people for directions, we'd feel flushed with victory when we finally located the bookstore.

After a search of bookstores in several towns, we deduced that the book was no longer in print. But that wasn't the end of it. A used-books seller suggested we try the local library. After a great deal more searching for the building itself in a labyrinth of twisting streets, we squeezed our car into a parking space several blocks away. The librarian hunted for forty-five minutes trying to track the book down, but someone had misplaced it, and it was not to be found. However, this stop yielded us the publisher's name and the date of publication.

By this time, Jack had enlisted the help of a used-books seller, but a long-distance call to him yielded nothing—except the knowledge that the book was now a "collector's item" and should we perchance *find* one, it would cost a fortune!

Now mind you, we were *on vacation*. Jack wouldn't have spent that kind of time otherwise. But I learned something new about this man I've been married to for two-thirds of my life. Not only has he some bulldog or bloodhound tendencies, but he thought ferreting out that information was *fun*. (Fortunately, so did I—but for different reasons. To me it was fun to observe *him* having fun in this way. For him, the search itself was the enjoyment.)

When I asked why he was going to all this trouble for a book he didn't even know he'd want to *read* if he got it, he said, "When I've got the time, I enjoy the challenge."

Understand what I mean about vacations?

Truthfully, this search could have been *irritating* if I'd not loved this guy so much! (And if he didn't humor *my* "druthers" on a vacation too!)

Ah, yes. Vacations reveal a great deal about our divergent interests.

A woman who loves to play golf, hike, and sightsee marries a man who loves to browse antique bookstores.

A man who loves the woods, bed-and-breakfast places, walking in the rain, marries a woman who wants to enjoy being pampered in a huge resort hotel.

A doer marries a sitter.

The list goes on.

How do you make peace with contrasting interests? I mean *extremely* divergent ones?

Respect is no doubt the key ingredient. The importance of this cannot be overstated.

"Respect is not included in the marriage vows," writes Anne Gottlieb. "No illustrated books show how to achieve it. And yet it is central to a lasting, satisfying marriage."

She goes on to say:

> What is this thing called respect? It is not the same as admiration. "When you fall in love, you *admire* the other," says Dr. Alexandra Symond, associate clinical professor of psychiatry at the New York University School of Medicine. "You look *up* to someone—much the way a child idealizes a parent."
>
> "I have one patient whose husband loves sports, especially tennis," says Dr. Symonds. "She would prefer to go to the theater, or to stay home and read. She could simply say, 'We have different tastes.' Instead she says, 'How can he waste his time and money that way?' She puts him down."
>
> The put-down is the chief symptom—and weapon—of lack of respect, or contempt.
>
> . . . Respect, then, is appreciation of the *separateness* of the other person, of the ways in which he or she is unique.[1]

I have an inkling that true respect and criticism are mutually exclusive. I may not agree with your choice or ideas, but if I respect *you*, I'll respect those choices and ideas as well.

The second essential is compromise.

Compromise is a necessary and beautiful word in a relationship between two different people who love each other and want to continue to grow in that love. Both must make adjustments. Both must give in order for love and harmony to flourish.

Someone asked me if Jack and I had to *learn* how to take a vacation together. At first I said, "At this point in our lives, I'm not even sure." As we talked further, I realized, yes, we did have to learn. But now the adjustments we've made over the years enhance our times away a thousandfold.

I'm the one who will gather up all the folders on what to see, do, buy, explore. And I'm inclined to want to do them *all*.

Jack, who has meticulously planned the flights, car rental, and places to stay, then wants to (1) relax and (2) play golf. Sightseeing and doing all the things there are to do would be much lower on his list.

And then there's shopping (high on my list, not on his at all).

You can see, our interests have differed—and still do to a degree—in the way we approach a vacation. But because we love each other, we want the other to enjoy the time, and so, over the years, we've discovered the joy of compromise.

Now when we travel, I pick out a couple of high-priority things I want to see and do and tell Jack about those right up front. I also tell him other things I'd *like* to do during the week, but those are negotiable.

Then, too, after much trauma, tears, and terror, I've learned to play golf! Not only play, but *enjoy* it! Oh, I'll never play *well*, being the non-athletic person I am, but I really do take pleasure in it now. And that is one game where we can differ in ability and still have fun playing together.

There are days, of course, that I'll say, "I'll just ride along with you this morning," or "You go ahead without me because I need to do some shopping" (or reading, or working), but those episodes are infrequent because we love to be together even though our interests vary.

Sometimes, it isn't even that we *prefer* different activities, it is that we have dissimilar capacities for them. I can take in more sights than Jack can, for instance. He gets overloaded on beautiful views, sunsets, flowers, and so on, sooner than I do. But he has a greater tolerance for golf courses and spectator sports than I. And then there's shopping . . . .

Finally, we have found in the midst of individual pastimes, it is imperative to *develop more and more mutual pursuits*.

Often I think of marriage as two overlapping circles. Two whole complete individuals come together—and sometimes, especially at first, only a small part of their lives coincide.

Some couples are content—even happy—with little overlap. Their circles would look like this:

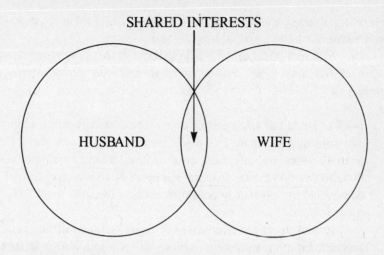

But for couples who want a deepening level of intimacy and togetherness, those circles must correspond more and more as the years go by to look like this:

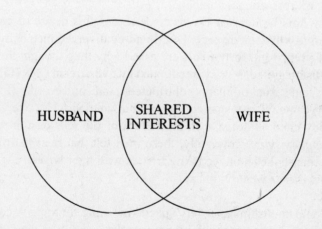

Never should those circles mesh completely and be identical. Each person will and should have separate interests to contribute to the overall growth and joy of a marriage. But the greater degree of overlap and the more we work at developing preferred activities together that will *ensure* that overlap, the closer we will come to having a deep, intimate relationship.

Dr. Willard F. Harley, Jr., a licensed clinical psychologist and author of *His Needs, Her Needs: Building an Affair-Proof Marriage*, comments:

> I define a need as what people enjoy tremendously when someone does that for them. I've discovered that in women, the primary needs are: affection, conversation, honesty and openness (a solid basis of trust), financial support (enough money to live comfortably), and family commitment (her husband must be a good father).
>
> Among men, the five basic needs are: sexual fulfillment, recreational companionship (having his wife join him in leisure activities), an attractive spouse (she tries to always look her best), domestic support (he finds peace and quiet at home), and admiration.[2]

Interesting that the second requisite in men, according to Dr. Harley, is "recreational companionship."

Dr. Lois Leiderman Davitz underscores this desire in an article concerning why men divorce. Four hundred divorced men between the ages of twenty and forty-five were asked why they thought their marriages disintegrated. Money (mentioned by five percent), sex (forty-nine percent said sexual problems contributed), and child-rearing (forty-two percent) came in for a share of course, but what virtually every man in her study cited as decisive in the failure of the relationship was *lack of companionship.* Universally, these men felt that their marriage fell apart because they stopped being friends with their wives.

Dr. Davitz went on to say,

> Companionship has a very special meaning for men. A companion is someone with whom you share activities that you enjoy. Almost all of these failed marriages, as reported by the men, involved very few shared activities. . . . Almost without exception, the men talked about their longing for a wife who would be a friend. "I wanted my ex to do things with me, show an interest in what I liked doing," says Larry, 36. "She hated my

motorcycle and accused me of using it as an escape to be with my buddies. I'd like her to know that my current girlfriend has her own Honda."

The men were equally clear about what companionship is not. It's not sex, though a desire for sex may grow out of companionship. It's not parallel activities, such as sitting together and watching TV. It's not necessarily outings with the children. Many men complained that all their recreation with their wives involved the entire family.[3]

A great many wives have never *seriously* thought about what constitutes companionship, or even friendship, for their husband or how he defines communication. Often she makes friends on the basis of commonality of feelings while he makes friends on the basis of commonality of activities. (Note Dr. Davitz's definition of a companion being "someone with whom you share activities that you enjoy.") His best buddy will be his business partner or the man he plays tennis with on weekends.

Communication to her involves sharing hearts. Communication to him involves discussing what has been done together.

Because of this, one counselor suggests that when things seem to be getting rocky, a woman needs to make an extra effort to do things *with* her husband. He says to try to include an activity *each day* that you both enjoy and carve out time to share it with him.

And *laugh* together! The divorced men who were interviewed consistently reported that they had fun with their wives less than once a month.[4]

Because some wives fail to understand how their husbands make and view friends, they don't see the importance of learning to enjoy what their husbands enjoy. Some say, "I can't." Others say, "Why should I?" Still others say, "What difference does it make?"

I think Dr. Harley and Dr. Davitz give us answers to the last two. And God gives us the answer to the first.

I often wonder if women who say "I can't" have ever really made it a matter of prayer. I cling to the fact that our God will never give us a command that He won't give us the ability to carry out! And it isn't our husbands who say, "Adapt to your husband" (Ephesians 5:22, PH—one of the meanings of the Greek word for "submit"). It is *God*.

I am convinced that God has given women a unique ability to *adapt*, to change. But we rarely ask Him for His help in this area.

I have to tell you, I prayed a lot about graduating from spectator to participant in sports. I don't like to be humiliated any more than anyone else! (And *still* I have to say to myself, "Carole, your self-worth is not bound up in how you play golf!"—because if it were, I wouldn't *have* any!)

When Jack and I first realized that one of the weakest areas of our marriage was recreational intimacy, we explored sports that we might play together and decided on tennis. Jack had played tennis in high school; I'd never owned a racket.

I had to pray for two things: First, that I'd like it—because I knew I'd never pursue it if I hated it. Second, that I'd have enough ability not to disgrace us both.

God answered. I loved it! And by taking lessons and practicing, I got so I could play a pretty good game of mixed doubles with Jack—and it added a new interest for us so that we both enjoyed watching professional tennis as well.

Then Jack injured his knee—weak from an old skiing accident—and he couldn't play tennis anymore.

Then I took up golf. I had to ask the Lord for the same two things, and God has answered—well, at least the first one.

If He can do it for me, wives, He can do it for you!

So keep learning. Keep growing. I feel that some new interest—*not previously explored*—should be added to our lives every few years. It can be a hobby, a course taken together, a sport, a board game, a new outreach such as teaching a Sunday school class together.

Obviously, this is a two-way street. A husband should learn to enjoy what his wife enjoys as well. Both partners should work at stretching their horizons.

I have to admit there are some things I'd have a harder time adjusting to than others. I'm glad Jack doesn't hunt. And I'm glad he doesn't like to watch wrestling. (Whew!)

But I am convinced should he enjoy even *those*, God could help me like them. After all, God made me to be Jack's wife and therefore can help each of us "fit."

But of course, then there's shopping . . . .

NOTES:

1. Annie Gottlieb, "The Heart of Every Successful Marriage," *Readers Digest* (April 1988), page 33.
2. "Building An Affair-Proof Marriage," interview with Dr. Willard F. Harley, *Contact* (June-July 1987), page 15.
3. Lois Leiderman Davitz, "Why Men Divorce," *Gazette Telegraph* (April 7, 1987).
4. Davitz, "Why Men Divorce."

24

Trading Places

THE SPIRITUAL GIFTS OF MERCY
AND LEADERSHIP

JACK

"Mommy," queried the small boy, "what do you say when you get married?"

"Oh," his mother replied offhandedly, "you say things like you promise to honor and be kind and loving."

A tiny frown appeared on her son's face as he said slowly, "Then—then you're not *always* married, are you?"

If keeping those wedding vows were the criteria, most of us would be in trouble! And perhaps one of the reasons why we aren't always kind and loving is because we don't understand our partner's spiritual gifts.

Multiple questions pound like waves on the shoreline: Are all spiritual gifts equally distributed among males and females? Or do men more often have the gift of administration and leadership, and women more often the gift of helps? Can a man have the gift of mercy and still be a strong leader? Can a woman have the gift of leadership and still be a supportive wife?

To explore all the hidden crevices in the landscape of spiritual gifts is not our aim. But we *would* like to explore two areas that are potentially confusing and seem to cause trouble more often than the rest. These two are the gift of mercy in men and the gift of leadership in women.

The Gift of Mercy in Men

Husband, if you have the gift of mercy, you hold a priceless gift within your hands. You empathize with hurting people; sympathize with others' problems; feel as they feel; are sensitive to needs that others may not notice. You are often tender, kind, and a peacemaker, and Christ has called you blessed.

But hold your gift with caution as well as awe. Thank God for it, but realize that each gift, if not used wisely, carries the potential of destruction. Maybe, *especially* yours.

As a peacemaker, you may shrink from confronting, from disciplining, from correcting. You may not handle negative emotions well and may tend to avoid conflict of any kind at any place in any way.

But while confronting may continue to be difficult for you, don't despair. You have the Holy Spirit to give you the strength to do what's needed—and God no doubt gave you a wife who has a gift that will help to make up what you lack in other areas of life.

Nevertheless, look long and hard at your gift of mercy. Here and now ask God for some *determines*.

First, *determine* to learn how to correct when appropriate, confront when necessary, discipline when required, and work through conflict *even if it kills you.*

Second, *determine* to use your gift within parameters. Two boundaries are critical. You must use all caution to keep yourself from becoming emotionally depleted or emotionally entangled.

Emotional depletion comes because you give so much of your emotional self away, it leaves you with little or nothing for yourself or for those dearest to you. This can cause depression and burnout.

Emotional entanglements lead to worse.

With tears in her eyes, a wife told us, "My husband, in full-time ministry, counsels troubled women. Three times in the last few years, he has become so emotionally involved with some of these women that it has almost destroyed our marriage and his ministry."

Over and over we hear it: "There is nothing physical going on between us. What can possibly be wrong in this relationship? That person is my friend and needs my support."

The danger of becoming emotionally involved with a person of the opposite sex is great. What starts out to be a helping friendship often turns into emotional entanglements that lead to destruction and despair. The danger is especially great with those people who have the gift of mercy.

Over lunch, a Christian leader told us of interviewing over two hundred Christian pastors and full-time workers who had become involved in adultery. He startled us by saying, "One of the most common denominators among these men who had affairs was that in over eighty percent of the cases, it started as a result of counseling the woman with whom they became involved."

Therefore men, *determine* one thing: be *wary* of counseling women. Some of you may need to determine *never* to counsel women, or only when your wife is present. Our friend who had done the survey pointed out that in Titus 2, Paul admonished Titus to teach older and younger men, but to "teach the older women . . . to teach what is good. Then *they* can train the younger women" (Titus 2:3-4, emphasis mine). Titus wasn't to teach or train the younger women himself. What a word of caution! And his teaching of the "older women" was probably not one to one.

A man with the gift of mercy can be an able leader in the family and in the church—a strong, sensitive, listening leader. Yes, he will need an extra measure of help from God to develop the ability to take firm stands, confront, and discipline, but he will likely discipline in love. However, he must remember the "determines" because frequent dangers await—the depletion of his own resources, neglect of family, and the great pitfall of emotional entanglements.

I hope you wives who are married to a man with the gift of mercy are not despairing. Sure, you may find yourself in the more active posture when handling tasks or challenges with the children's schooling or around the home, for example, persistent salesmen. You may be the one who insists on working through conflict issues to resolution even when emotions run high. But your understanding of this gift God has given your husband is crucial. Concentrate on looking at his thoughtfulness, his sensitivity to you and others, his ability to put himself in your shoes, his kindness and sweetness of spirit. Then praise God for these characteristics. Your husband's gift of mercy does not mean he is lacking in leadership. And in all probability, God has given you gifts with which to help and complete your husband—perhaps even gifts of exhortation or administration.

Often that's the way God fits us together. Let's hope that we *do* have different gifts so we can be much more as a couple than we could be alone. But unless we understand each other's spiritual gifts and the implications of those gifts, we often come to wrong and painful conclusions.

The Gift of Organization or Leadership in Women

The other patch of the landscape we want to explore is women who have the gift of leadership and organization.

Some men wish that women had only the invisible gifts. For them, it's acceptable for a woman to have the gift of serving. No problem with cooking meals for neighbors, sitting with the sick, offering to drive a friend to the airport, being available to help in a multitude of ways (that is, if it doesn't interfere with the husband's plans). According to them, the gift of hospitality for women is not only suitable, it's coveted. And he hopes she'll also have the gift of encouraging, the gift of mercy, the gift of contributing to the needs of others—perhaps even the gift of wisdom, if it isn't too noticeable. The gift of faith? Well that's okay if she doesn't make waves or make him feel inferior.

But what if she has the gift of leadership? Of teaching? Of administration? What then?

I am convinced with all my heart that one of the responsibilities of a husband is to know his wife's gifts and help her develop and use those gifts for Christ and His Church. God didn't create women and give them gifts just to serve *husbands*. To keep those gifts hidden within the walls of our homes; to trample and squash them; to say they aren't valid because they are too visible—is to rob God, His body, *and* the wife. We need to help her find God's will in using those gifts. *If we don't*, as leaders in our homes, it is *sin*.

We need to protect her, of course. Guide her, yes. But gentlemen, we also need to *turn her loose upon a needy world*.

Some wives have the gift of organization. They can manage everything from the checkbook and finances, to a conference for five hundred people, to Daily Vacation Bible school, to church programs, to a large office complex. Some husbands are so intimidated by their gifted wives, they fail to delegate even the handling of finances, thinking that if they do, they won't be the head of their home. What nonsense! A part of headship is taking responsibility for and developing other's gifts; then delegating responsibility to ones who are more gifted in a particular way than you are. It is discerning potential and figuring out ways to develop and use it.

But that can threaten us, can't it? We wonder if we turned them loose, would they manage *us* as well . . . would they take control of the home and become the head of the family?

That *is* a danger. If the wife doesn't put her gift into the hands of the Lord to use as He will; if she doesn't see her priorities as God sees them; if she has the idea that her gift makes her superior; then yes, her precious gift from God can be used wrongly and hurtfully.

But let's take a real-life situation.

Mary and Jim have three children—two of school age and one in preschool. Mary has the gift of leadership and has been asked to be the director of women's ministries at the church. They could use the extra money but realize that the decision shouldn't be based on that. Mary feels that she could give part time to the women's ministry and still handle her responsibilities as wife and mother. What should Jim and Mary do?

First, *ask God together* to find out His mind on this. That's so basic, isn't it? Yet we find that couples are doing that last instead of first and basing decisions on the pros and cons instead of on the will of God. It's one reason we get into so much trouble sometimes. God has said, "I will lead you and guide you in the way you should go." Pray about it individually and together until you are both convinced of His plan.

Second, *if God says yes* then other questions have to be answered. For instance, what responsibilities around the home should Jim assume in order to enable Mary to add this ministry to her schedule? If the need to do this bothers Jim, he must come to terms with the fact that he is doing this in *obedience* to God. His tasks around the home are for God as well as for Mary and the family.

Mary needs to ask some questions, too, such as: "What are my priorities? How can I ensure that I am keeping things in order of priority while adding this ministry? In what areas could it get out of balance? When would I know that? What might be a creative alternative for using my gift and still maintain my priorities? How can I be a supportive wife with a quiet and gentle spirit while I'm using this gift of leadership?"

Now, a wife doesn't have to go outside the home in order to use her gift of leadership, of organization, or of teaching. In a sense, a person with these gifts will be using them all the time whether she realizes it or not. She will use them in organizing her home, keeping the books balanced, and teaching her children. Her gift affects the way she approaches everything. One author put it this way:

> My own personal gift is *ruling* (leadership, administration) which means that I *approach* all of my family, business, and church situations in the same manner. Basically, this means that I have the ability to see the overall picture in just about any project I am confronted with or a part of. I have the ability to organize people and projects so that the task can be accomplished in the most efficient manner possible, even delegating some or much to be done in order to set and attain completion goals.[1]

How foolish a husband would be to try to change *that* gift even if it were possible! Yet we observe husbands who would squelch this gift in their wives if they could. And some try so hard that the cost has been great—in their wife's emotions and their family's happiness. Further, they are robbing the Body of Christ.

Years ago, I realized that Carole had some gifts that she needed to develop. She loved to work with women to help them grow spiritually. By one definition, she has the gift of exhortation (or encouraging), which expresses itself through her desire to communicate in teaching, speaking, and writing. At that time, she was working with a few individuals, leading a small Bible study but mainly managing our household. Together we began to pray for a greater outreach for her, and I encouraged her in every way I knew how.

Shortly after that, God led her to a ministry on the North Shore of Chicago, which began with one woman, grew to twenty-five, then blossomed into developing leaders of Bible studies, until several hundred women were being helped spiritually. In turn, this led to speaking opportunities and, when we moved to Colorado, a writing ministry as well. And I am thrilled at what God has done.

To be honest, it has meant less time for gourmet meals and projects around the house than she used to do. There have been weekends when I find myself eating fast food alone while she's off speaking at a women's retreat. And I miss her. But I've encouraged her to use the gifts God has given her, so I rejoice with her and pray for her. I would be sinning before God not to help her do what God wants her to do.

On her part, she has tried to be careful to make me number one after God on her priority list—and shows me that in many ways. Our ministry together comes next, then our daughter and her family, our home, and friends. Actually, her personal ministry of speaking and writing are rather far down on her list, and a number of times we've discussed the balance of all of these for her.

You know, I've often wondered if some men's problem with their wife's gifts is because they feel that some gifts (perhaps the visible ones) are more important than others (the behind-the-scenes ones). If so, they need to gain insight through study of Scripture and pray for God's mind on His gifts to the body.

But also we see women who have these gifts—and are using them—who fail to make their husbands *feel* important. In some cases it isn't so much the gift of leadership or organization or teaching in a woman that intimidates a man, but the way she handles the gift, her priorities, and her husband. Some men feel their responsibility as head of their home has been usurped; that *they* are a second-class citizen; that their wife really is running the whole show.

God forbid that any wife should act or feel as if she is the one "in charge."

God Himself is the One in charge! And then God has given the husband the responsibility to be the head of his home, of his wife—to protect her, care for her, encourage her, love her and also to *lead* her.

One further question to consider: Is your *call of God* more important than using your spiritual gift? I think most of us would say, "Of course." Then consider what your call of God is. First it is to *know Him* and then to *grow to be Christlike*. Then, husbands, you have a call of God to love and lead your wife and family, which includes helping each family member to develop full potential to serve the Lord. Wives, you have a call of God to love and support your husband and be a godly mother, which means examining priorities for your life continually, recognizing the "seasons" of your life, knowing you serve God first of all in your call as a wife and mother.

We hear many confusing voices about this these days, but let me encourage you to throw out all your preconceived ideas and *go straight to His Word.*

God won't fail to answer your questions. That's His promise.

NOTE:
1. Pat Hershey Owen, *Seven Styles of Parenting* (Wheaton, IL: Tyndale House Publishers, 1983), page 12.

25

Give or Take

A WAY OF LIVING THE COMMITMENT

CAROLE

Takers.

Some are natural-born. Some are made. Some, Heaven forbid, are both. But *takers*, nonetheless.

Few of you reading this will think the word defines you. Neighbor down the block maybe. Relative. Husband or wife or child perhaps. But not *you*.

So let me ask you: Do most of your thoughts center around your own needs? When getting together with a friend, are you most eager to find out how your friend is doing, or most eager to tell that friend how you are doing and what your struggles are? Who talks most, and about what? How many questions do you ask concerning what is really going on with your friend? Is the majority of your prayer time spent on "gimme's"—on your own needs—or on the needs of others? Is a frequent thought, "If only I had . . ."? What needs does your spouse meet for you? Do you meet for your spouse? Do you know what your spouse's deepest needs are? How frequently do you offer to help others? How often do you think they should help you?

Perhaps answering these questions will help determine if you are a taker. But then, you may have become an adept deceiver—especially of yourself. So perhaps you'll want to ask your spouse or a close friend (one who will be honest with you) in order to find out their opinion. If they think—or you do—that you are primarily a taker, don't despair. God can help you change. In fact, He *will* help you change if you ask Him. For we must change. To complete each other throughout our lives requires that both of us—to some extent anyway—be *givers*.

I used to think that marriage was a fifty-fifty proposition. I have since discovered that a good marriage is really an all-or-nothing proposition with *each* partner being willing to give all—one hundred percent—the vast majority of the time.

✝ ✝ ✝

Cheryl, an attractive redhead, called me out of the blue. Her husband of eight years had just told her he didn't think he could continue in their marriage even though he loved her and their two small children. No, there was not another woman.

Cheryl cried *why?*

The signs and symptoms were all there. They'd been there for years. But Cheryl hadn't seen them.

Her husband, Bill, a sensitive and caring person, had lost his mother two years earlier after a five-year bout with cancer. His father, a dry alcoholic for eleven years, gave up on life and went back to drinking. Often Bill drove for two hours to find him, pick him up off the street, and take him to a detox center.

Following his mother's death, Bill refused to go to a family camp with his father and three sisters to work through the grief. Refusal wasn't like him, and his terse, "I *can't* do it" should have been clue enough that something deep was wrong. But Cheryl asked no questions.

The work around their several-acre place demanded his weekend time so he had no recreation or time for a hobby. He had no "space."

When he bought her a necklace for Christmas, she told him she didn't like it and exchanged it. He didn't say anything, but pain followed pain when she responded without enthusiasm to his promotion at work.

Among other things, she criticized his being overweight. Two weeks before she called our home, he'd said to her, "I've not been able to eat recently, and I've lost several pounds." She said, "Maybe your body is trying to tell you something," and dropped the subject.

Bill's emotional and physical resources had been slowly used up.

But Cheryl, so consumed with herself, didn't even look his way.

Emotionally and physically, Cheryl had always dumped on Bill. When he came home after an exhausting day, the first thing she did was to complain about *her* difficult day and shove the children into his care for the evening. At the very moment Cheryl was thinking, "Our marriage is a good one; what's there to work at?" her marriage was falling apart.

Coming home from a meeting one night, she found Bill on the couch with a woman friend of hers. In defense, he said, "I was telling her how I feel. You're never here when I need to talk." What he was really saying was, "You are not *here for me*."

Crying over the phone, Cheryl said, "I know now I was blind to his hurt and his need. I . . . I just didn't *understand*."

And so Bill left. Depleted, seeing no chance of help or support, convinced that Cheryl wouldn't or couldn't change, he felt he needed to retreat from life and saw no way out but divorce.

Cheryl was a taker. And Bill simply had nothing left to give.

I wonder how often it happens that one partner forsakes a relationship out of hopelessness—the hopelessness of having nothing left to offer.

There are, of course, different ways of giving up besides walking out. Living an independent life within the framework of the marriage vows, becoming a nonentity, working seventeen hours a day, allowing a hobby to take over a life—all of these can be ways of throwing in the towel.

But if we want to complete each other, if we want to reach into the other's deepest needs and seek ways in which to help, then we are going to have to learn about *giving*.

J. C. Pollock writes concerning Maria, the wife of Hudson Taylor:

> Hudson would lean hard on her, drawing vigor from her spiritual maturity, her tranquility and faith, her unwavering affection. She gave him and their work all she had, every ounce of strength, every thought that crossed her intelligent mind, all the force of her love. She allowed him to drain her, and if sometimes his demands were unconsciously selfish, she was no more aware of it than he.[1]

How often do we see this kind of giving in our "me" generation?

Catherine Menninger, wife of Dr. William C. Menninger, writes, "Too many wives (and I was one of the too many) expect a weary man to come home at night and make up for the monotony of their lives; they demand that he be wit, sage, comforter and counselor all in one. 'You owe me this!' they seem to say, instead of asking themselves, 'What can I contribute?'"[2]

Do you realize that the Bible never talks about the "blessing of taking"? However, it has a great deal to say about the joys of giving—giving of our means, giving of ourselves unselfishly, bearing one another's burdens and so fulfilling the law of Christ.

Often I need to be reminded of what Paul said:

Don't let the world around you squeeze you into its own mould, but let God re-mould your minds from within, so that you may prove in practice that the plan of God for you is good, meets all his demands and moves toward the goal of true maturity. . . . Don't cherish exaggerated ideas of yourself or your importance, but try to have a sane estimate of your capabilities by the light of the faith that God has given to you all. (Romans 12:2-3, PH)

In order to move toward the goal of true maturity, to grow in giving, stamp out our tendencies to be takers, and learn more about completing each other, we need to refocus our energies both on making our marriages and our marriage partners a *priority* commitment.

Counselor Barry Cavanagh of Sacramento, California, says, "A marriage needs attention—regular infusions of zest, innovation and mutual self-disclosure." He suggests that every couple ask themselves: "Is our marriage a priority commitment, or do we give it only the leftovers of our time and energy?"[3]

Oh, yes, there is a cost in keeping the marriage relationship vital and growing. And one of the prices paid is in *time.* It's a payment that can't be held back without devastating consequences.

So to continue ensuring a joyful relationship, or to return to a more loving relationship, decide here and now that you, as a couple, are going to pay the price in time. Commit yourself to that weekend without the children every other month; dedicate ten to twenty minutes a day for in-depth communication and/or prayer together; and *weekly*, or at least

bimonthly, have a real rootin'-tootin' bonafide genuine *date*
two of you go out all by yourselves. It doesn't matter if it ʊ ⌐ʊ⌐ ⌐ ⌐
little coffee shop for hot chocolate on a winter night. What matters is
that you spend a couple of hours of unpressured time being together.

Spending time in meaningful communication is a necessity in a
good marriage, but it takes more than just that to change from a taker
to a giver. It requires allowing God to change us from the inside out.
One Christian counselor states:

> It's been my experience that mirrors make better tools for change
> than chisels do. In other words, you and I need to be mirrors
> in our marriage relationship, mirroring God to those we care
> most about. How do we do that on a practical, day-to-day basis?
> The best way I know is to begin putting the fruits of the Spirit
> (Galatians 5) into practice. Sometimes the truth we reflect can
> inspire change in others. Just as often, practicing the fruits of
> the Spirit will change us, giving us more patience and, perhaps,
> longsuffering, and ease the irritation in a different but equally
> effective way.[4]

The only way I know to grow in love, joy, peace, longsuffering,
gentleness, goodness, and faith is by falling more in love with Jesus
through spending time with Him. Time in His Word. Time talking to
Him in prayer. Time worshiping and praising Him. Time letting Him be
involved in the moments of my life. This commitment is all important
to have the quality of life I desire.

But let's suppose you are the giver. Right now you are deep-down,
rock-bottom *tired*. You are used up. At your wit's end.

Consider these two questions:

1. *Could it possibly be that you haven't clearly communicated to
your spouse what you need?* In a way that your spouse can understand?
One counselor writes:

> Sometimes the biggest irritations in a relationship are really
> minor problems that aren't deeply imbedded personality traits
> at all. I remember one couple who came to me for marriage
> counseling only after they'd made trips to their respective law-
> yers. The wheels of divorce were already grinding forward.

After they shared their problems with me, I asked them individually to make a list of answers to one very simple question: "What is it he/she could do to change that would please you?" When I asked him, he said, "I like her just the way she is. She just doesn't like me."

So I was ready for a horrendous list from her. Here's what she said: "Number one, I want him to tell me that he loves me in front of other people sometimes. I would like him to say 'I love you' in public. Number two, I'd like him to touch me in public, not just in bed. He never touches me in public. And third, when he comes home from work, I want him to find me in the house and say hello to me before he starts fiddling with his computer."

I read the guy his wife's list, and he said, "Is that it? I can do that." And they walked out of my office hand in hand. That was ten years ago; today they're still married and doing fine.

I tell this story to say that sometimes change can result from something as simple as communication. . . . You might want to sit down . . . and each make your own lists.[5]

According to the *San Diego Tribune*, the average American married couple spends twenty-three minutes a week in dialogue (including time spent asking about the laundry, dinner, etc.). Now I ask you, how are you going to make a marriage work in twenty-three minutes a week?

2. *Could it be that you aren't letting God fill you up with Himself?*
One of the passages I come back to time and time again is Ephesians 3:14-20 in *The Living Bible*. Listen closely with all your heart. God is talking to *you*:

When I think of the wisdom and scope of his plan I fall down on my knees and pray . . . that out of his glorious, unlimited resources he will give you the mighty inner strengthening of his Holy Spirit. And I pray that Christ will be more and more at home in your hearts, living within you as you trust in him. May your roots go down deep into the soil of God's marvelous love; and may you be able to feel and understand, as all God's children should, how long, how wide, how deep, and how high his love really is; and to experience this love for yourselves, though it is so great that you will never see the end of it or fully know or understand it. And so at last you will be filled up with God himself.

Now glory be to God who by his mighty power at work within us is able to do far more than we would ever dare to ask or even dream of—infinitely beyond our highest prayers, desires, thoughts, or hopes.

To be filled up with God Himself.
Giver, you'll always have more to give.

Taker, take hope. When you are filled full with God Himself, you will no longer need the last drops from the resources of others. Being filled with Him, having all the riches that are in Christ Jesus at your disposal, opening your heart wide to the incredible blessings of the Triune God, you'll find yourself—maybe slowly, but oh, so surely—becoming a *giver*.

And so . . . a completer.

NOTES:
1. J. C. Pollock, *Hudson Taylor and Maria*, page 172, quoted in *Restoring Your Spiritual Passion* by Gordon McDonald (Nashville: Oliver-Nelson, 1986).
2. Catherine W. Menninger with Margaret Lane, "What Wives Can Do to Solve the Communication Problem," *Readers Digest* (July 1969), pages 211-212.
3. Norman M. Lobsenz, "Ten Questions Couples Ask Marriage Counselors Most," *Readers Digest* (June 1976), page 72.
4. "Question and Answers," *Partnership* (January-February 1988), page 12.

26

Of Dollars and Sense
HOW WE LOOK AT MONEY

JACK AND CAROLE

One of our favorite lines in the Pooh books is a lament by the sad-faced donkey, Eeyore, as he looks at his reflection in a pond: "Pathetic! That's what I am. Pathetic!"

That line came to mind as we contemplated a great many attitudes concerning money. They are pathetic!

"The handling of finances," states David Augsburger, "is one of the major emotional battlegrounds of any marriage."[1]

Battlegrounds. The clashes range from small skirmishes to out-and-out war. Some are brief, well-defined flurries. Others are the surprise attacks of guerrilla warfare, or just another chapter of a long, organized, and sustained campaign. Peace treaties are infrequent. Negotiations? If you even get to the bargaining table. It can be dirty fighting out there!

Lack of finances is seldom the issue. "The root problem seems to be an unrealistic and immature *view* of money. Money can be used as an emotional instrument to control or manipulate and thus becomes the ultimate secret weapon, or it can be utilized as a way of compensating for deep inadequacies that we can't really confess or identify within ourselves."[2]

People too often believe the old adage called "The Golden Rule of Money": "He who has the gold makes the rules."

Question: What does money mean to you—*really*?

We all have key attitudes about money—but that doesn't mean that we're aware of them all! Test your attitudes: for instance, do you agree or disagree with the following statements?

- Money is the measure of success.
- Investments should be safe. I don't want to lose any sleep over them.
- It's better to give money than to receive it.
- Everything material that I need I have.
- Success isn't in acquiring something, but in getting it as a bargain.
- Money can solve most problems.
- Saying "no" to a money request makes me feel guilty.
- Money is the key to survival in this dog-eat-dog world.
- Money is the reward. No money is the punishment.
- Power is in the holder of the purse strings.
- I wish I had more money so I could give more away to charities.
- It's easier to get money than love.
- Money in the bank means security.[3]

You might want to answer the above separately from your spouse, then compare responses for discussion. You might be surprised!

Let's try something. Stare for sixty seconds at this word:

MONEY

Now write down the words that come to your mind—or pick from the following:

envy	lust	fulfillment
fear	scorn	useful
guilt	power	leisure
dreams	goals	responsibility
status	fun	serious
security	joy	give
temptation	control	hope

The words you choose may be a clue to what money means to you as an individual and help you to untangle your own attitudes about it. Does it mean security? Stability? Status? Freedom? Fulfillment of dreams? Or is it a way to express yourself, to have fun, to be generous? Or perhaps you look on it as something of a temptation that could confuse your priorities, and you're a bit afraid of its lure.

What money means to me affects my choices. If money means fulfilling dreams and I define my dream as a colonial two-story dream home, I may scrimp and scheme to get things for that house at the expense of a vacation with my family or a better school for my children. Or money may be security for me, and so I nag my husband to work at two jobs and then become depressed because he spends so little time with me.

My first responsibility, then, may be to ask God for wisdom as I examine my own heart to see what money really *does* mean to me.

And then what do I do with that information?

First, I ponder it until I come to an understanding of myself.

Second, I challenge my own thinking and examine it in the light of God's Word.

What is just "different" between my spouse and me, I accept.

What is wrong with my thinking, I change.

What is false in my partner's thinking, I take to God in prayer.

It's no wonder most of us come to marriage with some bad ideas about money. We've been brainwashed by the world, which says grab it, steal it, take it away from someone else, scheme for it, manipulate someone to get it, hoard it, flaunt it.

But God says earn it honestly, give generously, save for the future, use it wisely. We really must hold material things with an open hand so He can remove or give as He chooses. We must heed what Jesus said:

"You cannot serve two masters: God and money. For you will hate one and love the other, or else the other way around.

So my counsel is: Don't worry about things—food, drink, and clothes. For you already have life and a body—and they are far more important than what to eat and wear. . . . Will all your worries add a single moment to your life? . . .

Don't store up treasures here on earth where they can erode away or may be stolen. Store them in heaven where they will never lose their value, and are safe from thieves. If your profits are in heaven, your heart will be there too." (Matthew 6:24-25,27; 6:19-21, TLB)

Before we look at how attitudes and personality traits affect our view of material things, let's look at some rules for honor on the battle-field, or "How to Fight Fair About Finances."

We'll start with a "never"—*Never try to work through money problems while angry.* Calm down, then make an appointment with each other to try again. When you meet for that appointment, try incorporating some of the suggestions in this list.

Listen carefully to the other's suggestions without putdowns.

Read what other people have tried, such as the one-income family who sets aside two budget categories under the wife's man-agement—one for all household needs and the other for herself to spend as she sees fit. This helps her avoid the guilt involved when she's forced to choose continually between groceries and her own clothing items. Another one-income couple avoids conflict by having all the income under the wife's management. She pays all the bills and divides any remaining funds. This couple feels that this arrangement gives the woman more freedom to fulfill her role as manager in the family while maintaining her personal dignity.[4]

And now some "always" ground rules.

Always take time to discuss and thoroughly understand your income, insurance plans, investments, and assets as a couple. Put this on your "every six months" agenda.

Always try to understand your spouse's hidden agenda in money fights. Don't worry if you must agree to disagree. Studies show that unless one partner feels a need to totally dominate, agreeing to disagree doesn't mean you can't work together.

Whether joint account or separate, *always set aside a monthly amount of personal spending money for each of you.* Even a dollar will help!

A joint account has always worked best for us. From the beginning of our marriage, we prayed for the attitude of "What's mine is *ours*" and God has enabled us to feel that way. Even though there have been times when one of us has written a check and forgotten to record it, times of seeing that check returned with a NSF written in red ink across it, and times of despairing that we'd *ever* learn, we still feel that this arrangement reduces the potential for conflict.

But the important thing is not whether you have one account or two. It is, rather, the love that is shared in mutual trust of each other—and in trust of God.

To help foster and maintain that unity in financial matters, *let the books be open.* One of the easiest ways to create problems for each other is withholding information. When partners refuse to confide matters that are important to both, then all sorts of misunderstandings spring up.

Another essential guideline is, *make mutual decisions.* We have a rule at our house that any purchase over fifty dollars (Christmas can be an exception) has to be agreed upon. It used to be *much* less! But a working plan, a system of priorities, and an outline for the future is crucially important—probably even more important than a budget, because it discusses the *values* you want in life, not just "what" and "how" you go about buying. Call it a working attitude toward life, a common understanding on values and priorities, a plan for Christian stewardship. But whatever you call it, work at setting long-term financial goals in choosing a lifestyle that is really worthy of the kind of life you want to live—and God wants you to live—together.

Often the question comes, which spouse should handle the money? Well, the one who has that gift, of course! And husbands, remember that handling the money has nothing to do with God's declaring you to be head of the home.

I love this statement on money matters in marriage:

It's high time for Christians to choose to travel light. It is time to sort out our values and to pare those we keep down to the core, and to put the long-term eternal values in first place.

And so as husband and wife, choose values that are worthy of people who want to live the Jesus way in life—simply, openly, honestly, putting persons first. That might help money mean some of the same things to you both in your marriage.

Money can be the major problem in marriage—because of all its many mingled and mixed meanings. That is, *unless.* Unless communication worms its way through the emotional thicket of financial dreams, of wild expectations, of spending habits, and of our values, and our wants and needs. And it can be a major problem *until*. Until understanding tears out some of the underbrush of tantalizing attractions, of seductive appeals to consume, of compulsive needs to compete with other couples.[5]

Money. The responsibility of handling it is awesome. The call to use it wisely is great. The service it renders is incredible. And let me tell you, if you'll let God into that area in your life, you may never again have to say with Eeyore, "Pathetic! That's what I am."

Your profits will be in Heaven, and so will your heart.

NOTES:

1. Radio broadcast by David Augsburger, "The Meaning of Money in Marriage," *The Mennonite Hour* (Harrisonburg, VA 22801), #342-Money, Values.
2. Augsburger, "The Meaning of Money in Marriage."
3. These questions are taken from "Marriage and Money," *Partnership* (Spring 1988), page 32.
4. "Marriage and Money," page 32.
5. Augsburger, "The Meaning of Money in Marriage."

27

Gone Today or Here Tomorrow?

SPENDERS VS. SAVERS

JACK

The tiny furrow in Carole's brow deepened as her expression changed from questioning to disagreeing. I read the signs well. Sometimes her Dutch ancestry shows in the set of her jaw.

"But . . ." she said, and I could tell the discussion was escalating rapidly, "I'd like for us to pay their way. . . ."

"Honey," I reasoned, "we can't afford it."

"Well, we can afford it better than they can," she insisted.

I bit back a sharp retort, paused to send up a short word of prayer, and then said, "Sweetheart, we can't play God."

She knew what I meant. We'd discussed this dilemma before. Carole gets so emotionally involved in someone's problem that she wants to help whether it makes sense or not. Whether we really *can* or not. Whether we *should* or not. There are times when it is easier to help people simply by making the decision ourselves than by making sure we get God's leading on it. Carole tends to move quickly. I tend to wait and pray—and sometimes I probably do not move quickly enough.

We're not the only ones who approach finances from different sides of the court. This paragraph opened a recent article:

I am a grasshopper—the live-for-today spender. My husband, Don, is an ant—always saving "just in case." We had our first quarrel over money the month after we were married—when we got our first round of bills. He was convinced we'd be in the poorhouse by thirty. I was convinced he didn't love me.

Don and I aren't alone. I think of the statement, "Money isn't everything, but it's way ahead of whatever's in second place." Not very Christian, perhaps—but its sentiments ring true with many couples in conflict. Recent surveys in *Money* magazine and *Ladies' Home Journal* reveal that more couples fight about money than whatever is in second place (sex, kids).[1]

Quarrels about money sprout from many roots. However, as we mentioned in the previous chapter, the problems seem to lie not in how *much* money we have, but instead in how we *spend* the money we do have—on what, if we should, how much to give or save.

Many insist that a person's outlook on how money should be spent is strictly a matter of family background—how your family viewed and spent money. But I think this is only partly true.

CAROLE
I can vouch for that!

My brother Kent, my sister Muriel Joye, and I had completely different attitudes toward money from the start, yet we grew up with the same parents and family spending patterns.

We were each given an allowance.

I spent mine immediately . . . then asked for more.

Kent and Joye put theirs away, and expected needs and wants to be provided.

Kent and Joye relished counting what was in their piggy banks. I don't even remember having a piggy bank.

As I've gotten older, I've realized that although much of our attitude about money is learned, a great deal is also inherent in our personality.

JACK
To one, money is for *using*.

To another, money is for *having* so you can use it later.

One cries "give."

The other cries "keep."

The giver thinks the saver is stingy, miserly, selfish.
The saver thinks the giver is foolish, unwise, unthinking.
And in extremes, each is *right* about the other.

Even within the categories of savers and spenders, few are consistent. Carole's dad was a saver and would only replace a threadbare suit with the greatest reluctance and under extreme pressure from her mom, but he was generous with the family, in giving to the Lord, and in gift giving.

However, it's the savers who take the attitude, "Let's think about this—we don't want to waste money." They consider money *serious.* It is *security* and it calls for *responsibility.*

To the spenders, *budget* can be a dirty word. To them, money is *freedom* and *independence* and *fun.*

Words of a Saver	Words of a Spender
careful	freedom
serious	independence
security	fun
responsibility	easy come/easy go
budget/lists/accounts	*(but if it's not there, I won't spend it; no big deal)*

We grimace with pain at the thought of the difficulties that arise when a saver marries a spender (and it rarely fails!), but I wonder if a couple won't have to deal with as many problems if they are alike in this area.

If two radical spenders marry, they will end up quarreling about which creditors to pay first! And if two extreme savers wed, they'll no doubt fight about whether to take a cheap vacation and when to replace a sagging mattress.

The way we are wired together no doubt helps determine in which direction our current runs. But whether our attitudes come from our background, examples, convictions, or personality, one imperative need is to figure ourselves out and then untangle the complex views of our spouses. For this, understanding and balance are the key.

The Bible paints a picture of the perfectly balanced life in every area—and attitudes about money are no exception. Scripture lauds both the giver and the saver. Of the giver, Paul says, "Whoever sows sparingly will also reap sparingly, and whoever sows generously will also reap generously. Each man should give what he has decided in his heart to give, not reluctantly or under compulsion, for God loves a cheerful giver" (2 Corinthians 9:6-7). This, of course, is talking about giving to others, not spending on ourselves.

Then the teacher in Proverbs counsels, "A good man leaves an inheritance for his children's children," and "Go to the ant, you sluggard; consider its ways and be wise! . . . It stores its provisions in summer and gathers its food at harvest" (13:22 and 6:6-8).

But most of us are *un*balanced in this area. Those of us who focus on the here and now need someone to help us see beyond the present moment and look for larger meanings in life. The future-oriented among us need someone to help us be open to the blessings each day brings and to learn the joy of living one day at a time.

Stability and maturity in our views of money will bring glory to God. And that's our goal, isn't it?

Misers don't reflect His glory. Spendthrifts don't either.

Excesses are never a part of the balanced Christian life.

But let's walk another step.

One of the most crucial lessons concerning money is what God wants to teach us through it—and that includes through the *lack* of it. He longs for us to know that it is He who provides, and therefore He should be the one to decide how the money is spent.

Carole and I entered marriage with a similar attitude concerning money: an easy one of unconcern. If we had it, we spent it. If we didn't have it, we'd charge it and worry about it later. Oh, we weren't overly extravagant. For our first four years, we lived in a twenty-eight-foot trailer, rarely bought clothes, and never dined at expensive restaurants. Our big night out was a one-dollar spaghetti dinner at Sammy's and an evening listening to records at a department store. But we had fun! And sometimes we'd find ourselves working all summer to pay the previous year's Christmas bills.

During our first years out of seminary, God taught us some stern lessons. We cut up all credit cards and learned to make do with very little. If we had it, we still might spend it, but if we didn't have it, we bought *nothing*—including groceries. (God never let us starve but we did eat pancakes for one whole week!)

And God continued faithfully to teach us a Big Essential: *He provides*—but often not in ways we thought He would, or even should.

CAROLE
During that period in our lives, I found that I tried to tell God what would bring glory to His name . . . in many areas. But especially in the area of finances.

Parachurch groups often operate differently than does a church. Instead of a regular salary guaranteed by a congregation, a budgeted salary is paid to workers only as the money comes in from those to whom the person or group has ministered.

God led us to serve with such an organization, and it was often an exciting and scary adventure to see how the bills were going to be paid.

In early February 1963, Jack came home from a conference for two days, and then left for a two-and-a-half-week ministry trip. He needed what little money we had for gasoline, but the rent was overdue and there was no money left to pay it.

Jack and I had been tested many times concerning finances, but this was the first time that I faced an overdue rent payment all by myself. We had prayed much about it and we both felt he should go on the trip, but I'll tell you, that rent payment loomed *large*. Besides the rent, our daughter, Lynn, badly needed shoes for school. On February 13 our "salary" check came—just enough to buy her some shoes and to pay two urgent personal bills. But not enough to pay the rent.

By the fifteenth, I was desperate! Yet God kept my heart at peace in a way I had never before experienced. I prayed every day for faith to trust Him another day, and He gave it. Finally ninety dollars came—half the rent. (You have to remember, this was 1963!) I sent it in with a note of apology saying I'd send the rest as soon as I could. Then—from someone we'd never heard from before—came a check for one hundred dollars. I cried for joy as I praised the Lord for His provision.

But I was concerned about paying that bill late and in two partial payments. I had been telling the Lord that I didn't think it was a very good testimony for Him to have us late with the rent. Get that? I had been telling Him!

Then, in response to my two notes of apology and the second half of the rent money, came a note from our Jewish landlord. He said,

"Thank you for your letters and consideration. If there were more people in the world like you, the world would be a beautiful place to live."

I had never even *met* this wealthy landlord! But God had used my notes—and the late payments that necessitated them—to, yes, *bring glory to His name.*

Who am I to tell *God* what will do that?

I think it was Hudson Taylor who once said, "Difficulties are a platform on which God can reveal Himself." In response to that I wrote, "I'm beginning to see what that means. If we never sorrowed, how could we know God as a God of Comfort; if we never had any dark valleys, how would He be revealed as the Light of life; if never any financial or other needs arose, how could we see Him as a God who will supply *all* our needs (Philippians 4:19)? So difficulties are (1) for our perfection—to let the 'scum' of our lives rise to the top and be strained out from the gold and (2) to show us more of God Himself. No wonder we should 'count it all joy.' That's easy to say when you aren't *in* the furnace, but hard to remember when the fire gets hot. Isn't it wonderful that God knows *that*, too?"

Finances—or lack of them—are the most concrete, wonderful way to learn that *God provides.*

JACK

We need also to learn that He should be the one to *decide* whether to spend that money, to save it, or to give it away. Even in the instance Carole mentioned, she had to pray for God's mind whether the money from that small salary check was to go for Lynn's shoes, the personal bills, or part of the rent.

If a husband and wife really want God to decide about spending and are attuned to His voice, money arguments wouldn't be so common-place, would they?

Yet couples often hear God differently, and so we must go one final step.

At the wedding of a friend's daughter one Saturday morning in June, we found ourselves sitting next to a Christian financial counselor whom we had known years ago. Before the ceremony began, I asked him, "In your financial counseling, what is the most recurring difficulty couples have?"

Without a moment's hesitation, he said, "Stewardship."

"What do you mean?" I queried.

"Most Christian couples I talk to do not really understand that all they have is God's and that they are only *stewards* for Him. They may know this intellectually, but it hasn't become a part of their attitudes or lives. Consequently, they get themselves into debt, quarrel about money, and spend excessively on themselves. I am convinced that if we could get people to understand the truth of the fact that *all they have belongs to God* and they are only stewards handling *His* property, most of their problems would be overcome."

At that point the strains of the wedding march began and we fell silent. But my mind kept probing the truth of what he'd said.

A "steward" is a person put in charge of the affairs or the estate of another, including supervision and management of accounts. The steward acts as an administrator of finances and property for another. To be good stewards in our Christian lives, then, means that we realize deep within us that we are only managers and administrators for what belongs to God and is temporarily loaned to us.

God tells us to be *good* stewards—of our time, our talents, our possessions. But in reality, they are His time, His bestowed talents, His possessions—and not ours at all.

I was struck recently with the way King David viewed what God had given him. David was overwhelmed that he had the awesome privilege of having *anything* to give back to the God who already owned it. Listen to what David says:

> But who am I, and who are my people, that we should be able to
> give as generously as this? Everything comes from you, and we
> have given you only what comes from your hand. We are aliens
> and strangers in your sight, as were all our forefathers. . . . O
> LORD our God, as for all this abundance that we have provided
> for building you a temple for your Holy Name, it comes from
> your hand, and all of it belongs to you. (1 Chronicles 29:14-16)

Perhaps many of our struggles, quarrels, contentions, and thinking patterns concerning finances are due not to the money itself, but rather to our *view* of it. Even if we aren't battling debts or quarreling about money, all of us need to know what God's Word says concerning His view of material things. You might like to begin by reading Richard

Foster's powerful book called *Money, Sex, and Power* and then either do some topical studies through Scripture or work through some books and studies on finances by Larry Burkett, George Fooshee, or Ron Blue.

Please don't delay. Although some quarrels are caused by ignorance of your partner's personality as it regards money matters and others may be caused by an imbalance and immaturity in this regard, first and foremost may be a wrong view of who owns it in the first place. Our problems here are often a result of a distorted view of *stewardship*.

Understanding your spouse will help you.

Using the varying gifts of each will enable you.

But ultimately, it sifts down to three truths that God's Word will teach you, which must *grip your soul*.

God provides.

He should decide.

All of it belongs to Him.

That's what stewardship is all about.

NOTE:
1. Lynda Rutledge Stephenson, "Why Couples Argue About Money," *Marriage Partnership* (Spring 1988), page 30.

28

Look Straight Ahead
THE IMPERATIVE OF FAITHFULNESS

JACK

Hearing your name paged at the airport between flights on your way home from a long-distance trip is scary. I answered the page with trepidation.

It was a longtime friend of mine. "Jack, I'm here at the airport and I need to see you."

After arranging to meet him at our departing gate, I closed my eyes and breathed a prayer for wisdom. I had talked to my friend's wife two weeks earlier and heard the pain in her voice as she told of her husband walking out on her, the family, and the church he pastored. He left with a married woman who had been serving as the church secretary.

Several minutes later I spotted him coming toward me—and emerging from the crowd along with him was the "other woman."

Carole and I spent the better part of the next three days doing everything we could to help these two people see the awfulness of what they were doing; to see the situation from God's point of view. But we failed. Our friend did go back to his wife for a short time, but even as he left me to head home, we knew it wouldn't work. He had not repented before God but had made up his mind he wanted his lover above everyone else. Though he went through some motions to seek counsel and get further help, he had already predetermined his course. Today he and the former church secretary are together—at the cost of two broken families, a son who has tried suicide, children who need the pieces put back together for them, a devastated church, and disgrace mantled on God's community.

This man used all the excuses that are prevalent today. Prevalent—and wrong!

"But it must be God's will," he said. "God wouldn't have put her in a place where I'd fall in love with her otherwise."

And yet he could quote by heart the Scripture:

When tempted, no one should say, "God is tempting me." For God cannot be tempted by evil, nor does he tempt anyone; but each one is tempted when, by his own evil desire, he is dragged away and enticed. Then, after desire has conceived, it gives birth to sin; and sin, when it is full-grown, gives birth to death. (James 1:13-15)

How many times I've heard that phrase, "It has to be God's will." And even, "God told me to do it."

This is said by the very people who have sometimes preached on 1 Thessalonians 4:3-8, which says plainly:

It is God's will that you should be sanctified [holy]; that you should avoid sexual immorality; that each of you should learn to control his own body in a way that is holy and honorable, not in passionate lust like the heathen, who do not know God; and that in this matter no one should wrong his brother or take advantage of him. The Lord will punish men for all such sins, as we have already told you and warned you. For God did not call us to be impure, but to live a holy life. Therefore, he who rejects this instruction does not reject man but God, who gives you his Holy Spirit.

That last verse in the Phillips version says, "It is not for nothing that the Spirit God gives us is called the *Holy* Spirit." I like that!

My pastor friend was violating several commands from this passage alone. He was not being holy, he didn't avoid sexual immorality, he wronged a brother, he rejected God's instruction, and in a very real sense violated God's *Holy* Spirit. Yet he had the audacity to stand there and say, "It must be God's will."

What has happened that so many are compromising with sin, disobeying God, seeming to turn their backs on all they have taught and lived for?

I don't have all the answers to that. The pressures of the age we live in are great. We, as a nation and as individuals, have moved away from what we once saw as sin—what *is* sin. Oh, now we call it by nicer names. A person is no longer promiscuous but "sexually active." A homosexual has a different "preference." Abortion is "freedom of choice." And adultery? Well, some would excuse it as *God's will*! Our Lord God must shudder.

When did we forget that God never said we must be happy? He said we must be obedient. He never said we'd have our fleshly desires satisfied. He told us to flee temptation, to resist the lusts of this world.

Thousands of years ago, Saul's kingdom was taken from him because of one act of disobedience. And when he tried to plead and make excuses, the prophet Samuel said, "Does the LORD delight in burnt offerings and sacrifices as much as in obeying the voice of the LORD? To obey is better than sacrifice, and to heed is better than the fat of rams" (1 Samuel 15:22). Today we might paraphrase that verse, "To obey is better than what we call happiness here and now; to heed His voice is better than satisfying the most intense desire of your flesh."

But somehow we think God is going to deal with our sin less harshly than He has in days gone by. We have been duped into thinking that the most important thing in our lives is to satisfy ourselves rather than to obey Him. Somehow we make light of heaping disgrace on His bride, His Body—the Church of Jesus Christ.

So what can we do to insure emotional and physical faithfulness for the rest of our life?

Don't play with fire or you will surely get burned. Did you know this common saying comes from the Bible? Proverbs 6:27-28 cautions, "Can a man scoop fire into his lap without his clothes being burned? Can a man walk on hot coals without his feet being scorched?"

Be tough on yourself on this one. Today we seem to think we can flirt with temptation with immunity. And that just isn't so!

I have a friend—a former "peace child" from the sixties—who

used to say often, "Oh, that's so *straight*," as though that were a disgusting thing to be. As she grew in the Lord, she finally concluded that what she was calling "straight," God called *obedience*. Proverbs uses this word *straight* concerning temptation: "Let your eyes look straight ahead, fix your gaze directly before you. . . . Do not swerve to the right or the left; keep your foot from evil" (4:25,27).

A godly friend of mine told of walking down the street in a foreign city where he knew no one. A beautiful girl walked by him and gave him a flirtatious look. He smelled her perfume, was aware of her beauty and her availability. And he knew if he *looked back*, he'd fall into sin.

So he *refused* to look back.

It's the second look, the second thought, the second conversation, after you are aware of how pleasing the *first* one is, that entices. So if you are determined to obey God in being faithful to your marriage vows, consider this advice:

Know you. self and your own limits. Put up boundaries around your heart and behavior that protect the ground reserved only for your spouse. Carole and I are careful to share our deepest feelings, needs, and difficulties with *each other*, not with friends of the opposite sex. If a friendship with someone of the opposite sex is meeting needs that your mate should be meeting, end it *now*, because whether you admit it or not you are playing with fire.

We have seen great unhappiness and harm caused to a marriage when one partner becomes emotionally involved with another person, even when it doesn't lead to physical involvement. And emotional involvement is such a subtle temptation that it creeps up from one's blind side unless we are aware and open to the voice of the Holy Spirit.

Ruth Senter wrote about her encounter and ensuing friendship with a Christian man she met in a graduate class. She told of her struggle and finally her godly response to this temptation as she wrote a letter ending the relationship in which she said, "Friendship is always going somewhere unless it's dead. You and I both know where ours is going. When a relationship threatens the stability of commitments we've made to the people we value the most, it can no longer be."[1]

Realize the power of your eyes. Your eyes, it's been said, are the windows to your heart. Pull the shades down if you sense someone is pausing a little too long in front of your windows . . . reserve the deep type of look for only one person.[2]

Remember to fear God! Yes, He is a God of love and compassion. Yes, He forgives. But it is important to *fear* God. The fear of God is often a deterrent in my life to sin. Frankly, I'm afraid of the consequences of my sin because God says that I'll reap what I sow. And I'll do it in this life.

God is not a benign entity who overlooks sin. He is holy, and He will discipline us because He loves us.

Have you already fallen? Go to the Father and confess your disobedience. Let Him wrap His arms of love and forgiveness around you. But remember, confession means *forsaking, turning around,* resolving not to do it again. If you've been unfaithful, the scars will remain but the wound can heal. It may take months, even years, but God can rebuild the waste places if you will let Him.

His is a promise that rings through time and eternity, "Now to Him who is able to keep you from stumbling, and to make you stand in the presence of His glory blameless with great joy, to the only God our Savior, through Jesus Christ our Lord, be glory, majesty, dominion and authority, before all time and now and forever. Amen" (Jude 24-25, NASB).

He can keep you from falling.

He can even keep you from *stumbling*!

Trust Him, and there you will find "great joy."

NOTES:

1. Ruth Senter, "Rick," *Partnership* (January-February 1988), quoted in *My Soapbox* (October 10, 1988).
2. Dennis Rainey, *My Soapbox* (October 10, 1988), newsletter published by Family Ministry, P.O. Box 23840, Little Rock, AR 72221-3840.

29

Thank God
We're Not Alike

A FINAL NOTE ON THE WAY WE ARE

JACK
The group had no sooner finished talking than he bolted up out of his chair as though his underside had been stung.

We'd been discussing the positives of being different and how rarely we find married couples who are alike. He obviously had a question he couldn't wait to ask me.

"But what if . . ." he began without preliminary. "Well, how do you counsel a couple who *are* alike?"

"In what way are they alike?" I asked.

"They're both objective, factual, logical people—like you. They go out to dinner and they're finished talking in five minutes!"

I grinned, then paused to think about his question. "Well, if they're both satisfied with that, maybe there isn't a problem." But I hesitated as another thought crossed my mind. "The one difficulty could be that they aren't learning to relate to the fifty percent of the people in the world who are different than they are."

He blinked and then nodded slowly. "Hmmm. That's right. She has a difficult time even listening to the problems of the women in her Bible study," and his eyes narrowed thoughtfully. "And of course, they don't like it when they don't seem to have much to talk about."

We've talked about the difficulties of differences. But I believe the difficulties of being *alike* are far more serious.

239

a couple were . . .

- both logical thinking types, we might be unaware of others' feelings.
- both "perceptives," we might leave most projects incomplete.
- both hard-driving cholerics, we might be workaholics who fail to enjoy life.
- both carefree artist-types, we might be poor planners or fail to take seriously what needs to get done.
- both sensing thinkers, we might drive others crazy with our meticulous programs.
- both introverts, we might never entertain.
- both from families who cared nothing for neatness, we might be slovenly.
- both perfectionists, we might be so fastidious that we'd forever be making others uncomfortable and ourselves unhappy.
- both easy-going, we might compromise on what is right.
- both extremely disciplined and independent, we might be adamant that we're *always* right.
- both dependent, we could fall apart in crises.
- both pessimists, we might worry all the time.
- both savers, we might be miserly.
- both spenders, we could end up in the poor house.

If a couple is alike, then the task of learning to relate to the total world will take far more effort. It is in the *kindness* of God that He gives to most of us the privilege to learn from the one we love the most on earth.

The Bible describes marriage as *two becoming one.* Two complete, whole individuals come together to form a new entity—a couple, a *partnership*—who together are far stronger than either one alone.

But not just stronger. *Better.* More complete. United. Compensating for each other's weaknesses, encouraging each other's strengths.

Marriage *is* all that if we'll let it become all that God intends.

If we really believe that God chose for us a person who was made to "fit" us (as someone said, not to give us fits, but to *fit* with us), to complete us, to fill in what is lacking, then we need to thank God for *not* making us alike even though those very differences can sometimes make marriage a bumpy ride. Without those bumps, the ride could be monotonous and dull.

Marriage is a crucible in which to be melted and then formed into the likeness of Christ. In this furnace, we are heated until we are melted down, repoured, and remolded, only to be melted, molded, and polished again and again.

We can resist God's process at any stage—but if we do, He finds a less-than-best melting pot in which to transform us.

Marriage *forces* change whether we like it or not; whether we approve or not; whether we consent or not. But if we resist, dig in our heels, refuse to give ourselves to the Master's craftsmanship, strange twists and shapes appear which must again be held to the fire.

May we hold our marriage with hands of love and concern. May we cherish it with faithfulness and perseverance. May we make our relationship a priority and maintain that relationship with vigilance. May our love grow into a reflection of Christ's love for His Church.

Until we join the Body of Christ as His bride and are wed . . .

To the Bridegroom.

"Be imitators of God, therefore, as dearly loved children and *live a life of love*, just as Christ loved us and gave himself up for us as a fragrant offering and sacrifice to God" (Ephesians 5:1, emphasis mine).

"Christ loved the church and gave himself up for her to make her holy, cleansing her by the washing with water through the word, and to present her to himself as a radiant church, without stain or wrinkle or any other blemish, but holy and blameless" (Ephesians 5:25-27).

Amen.

Appendix
THE MYERS-BRIGGS TYPE INDICATOR

We have taken the Myers-Briggs Type Indicator (MBTI) on two different occasions, and both times the outcome was the same. As a result of taking this inventory, studying the results, and continuing an ongoing discussion of what it revealed, we have learned much about ourselves and each other.

The MBTI is a questionnaire developed by Isabel Briggs Myers and her mother, Katharine C. Briggs, to facilitate application of C. G. Jung's theory of "psychological types." Myers described the essence of the theory as this: Apparently random variations in behavior are actually consistent and orderly when one understands differences in the ways people prefer to take in information and make decisions.

Understanding the Four Categories
The MBTI categorizes these differences according to four preferences—Extroversion and Introversion (EI); Sensing and Intuition (SN), which are the two kinds of perception; Thinking and Feeling (TF), which are the two kinds of judgment; and Judging or Perceptive (JP), which are attitudes for dealing with the environment. The four scores combine to generate sixteen types, each with its own characteristics and gifts, its own road to excellence, and its own pitfalls to avoid.

The MBTI is based on three primary assumptions:

1. true preferences actually exist;
2. persons can give an indication of the *preferences* that combine to form "type" on a self-reporting inventory;
3. the preferences are dichotomized (i.e., described in opposing pairs), and the two poles of each preference are equally valuable.

The MBTI does not try to measure people against a standard but to sort them into groups—to which, in theory, they already belong.

A. Sensing/Intuition (S/N).

The Perceiving Functions include two ways of perceiving or taking in information.

S The sensing function takes in information by way of the five senses—sight, sound, feel, taste, and smell.

N The intuiting function processes information by way of a sixth sense or hunch.

Both ways of perceiving and taking in information are used by everyone, but one is usually preferred and better developed.

SOME CHARACTERISTICS

Sensing	Intuition
Looks at parts and pieces	Looks at patterns and relationship
Lives in the present, enjoys what's there	Looks toward the future, anticipating what might be
Prefers handling practical matters	Prefers imagining possibilities
Likes things that are definite, measurable	Likes opportunities for being inventive
Starts at the beginning, taking one step at a time	Jumps in anywhere; leaps over steps
Reads instructions and notices details	Skips directions; follows hunches
Likes set procedures, established routine	Likes change and variety

S's may seem too materialistic and literal-minded to N's; N's may seem fickle, impractical dreamers to S's.

Sensing types use both S and N, but prefer S. Intuitive both S and N, but prefer N.

B. Thinking/Feeling (T/F).

The Deciding Functions are two ways of deciding or evaluating.

T The thinking function decides on the basis of logic and objective considerations.

F The feeling function decides on the basis of personal subjective values.

Both ways of deciding and evaluating are used by everyone, but one is usually preferred and better developed.

SOME CHARACTERISTICS

Thinking	Feeling
Decides with the head	Decides with the heart
Goes by logic	Goes by personal convictions
Concerned for truth, justice	Concerned for relationships and harmony
Sees things as an onlooker, from outside situation	Sees things as a participant, from within a situation
Takes a long view	Takes an immediate and personal view
Spontaneously finds flaws and criticizes	Spontaneously appreciates
Good at analyzing plans	Good at understanding people

T's may seem cold and condescending to F's; F's may seem fuzzy-minded and emotional to T's.

Thinking types use both T and F, but prefer T. Feeling types use both T and F, but prefer F.

C. Extroversion/Introversion (E/I).

The Focus Attitudes include two complementary attitudes toward the world.

E An extrovert's essential stimulation is from the environment, the outer world of people and things.

I   An introvert's essential stimulation is from within, the inner
world of thoughts and reflections.

Both attitudes are used by everyone, but one is usually preferred and
better developed.

SOME CHARACTERISTICS

Extrovert	*Introvert*
Feels pulled outward by external claims and conditions	Feels pushed inward by external claims and conditions
Energized by other people and external experiences	Energized by inner resources, internal experiences
Acts, then (maybe) reflects	Reflects, then (maybe) acts
Is often friendly, talkative, easy to know	Is often reserved, quiet, hard to know
Expresses emotions	Bottles up emotions
Needs relationships	Needs privacy
Gives breadth to life	Gives depth to life

E's may seem shallow to I's; I's may seem withdrawn to E's.
Extroverts use both E and I, but prefer E. Introverts use both E and
I, but prefer I.

D. Judging/Perception (J/P).
The Lifestyle Attitudes are two complementary lifestyles.

J   A judging lifestyle is decisive, planned, and orderly.
P   A perceptive lifestyle is flexible, adaptable, and spontaneous.

Both attitudes are part of everyone's lifestyle, but one is usually preferred and better developed.

SOME CHARACTERISTICS

Judging	*Perception*
Prefers an organized lifestyle—tends to organize what is important and may let other things go	Prefers a flexible lifestyle
Likes definite order and structure	Likes going with the flow
Likes to have life under control	Prefers to experience life as it happens
Enjoys being decisive	Enjoys being curious, discovering surprises
Likes clear limits and categories	Likes freedom to explore without limits
Feels comfortable establishing closure—getting something done	Feels comfortable maintaining openness
Handles deadlines, plans in advance	Meets deadlines by last minute rush

J's may seem demanding, rigid, and uptight to P's; P's may seem disorganized, messy, and irresponsible to J's.

Judging types use both J and P, but prefer J. Perceptive types use both J and P, but prefer P.

People Making A Difference

Family Bookshelf offers the finest in good wholesome Christian literature, written by best-selling authors. All books are recommended by an Advisory Board of distinguished writers and editors.

We are also a vital part of a compassionate outreach called **Bowery Mission Ministries**. Our evangelical mission is devoted to helping the destitute of the inner city.

Our ministries date back more than a century and began by aiding homeless men lost in alcoholism. Now we also offer hope and Gospel strength to homeless, inner-city women and children. Our goal, in fact, is to end homelessness by teaching these deprived people how to be independent with the Lord by their side.

Downtrodden, homeless men are fed and clothed and may enter a discipleship program of one-on-one professional counseling, nutrition therapy and Bible study. This same Christian care is provided at our women and children's shelter.

We also welcome nearly 1,000 underprivileged children each summer at our Mont Lawn Camp located in Pennsylvania's beautiful Poconos. Here, impoverished youngsters enjoy the serenity of nature and an opportunity to receive the teachings of Jesus Christ. We also provide year-round assistance through teen activities, tutoring in reading and writing, Bible study, family counseling, college scholarships and vocational training.

During the spring, fall and winter months, our children's camp becomes a lovely retreat for religious gatherings of up to 200. Excellent accommodations include heated cabins, chapel, country-style meals and recreational facilities. Write to Paradise Lake Retreat Center, Box 252, Bushkill, PA 18324 or call: (717) 588-6067.

Still another vital part of our ministry is **Christian Herald magazine**. Our dynamic, bimonthly publication focuses on the true personal stories of men and women who, as "doers of the Word," are making a difference in their lives and the lives of others.

Bowery Mission Ministries are supported by voluntary contributions of individuals and bequests. Contributions are tax deductible. Checks should be made payable to Bowery Mission.

 Fully accredited Member of the Evangelical Council for Financial Accountability

Every Monday morning, our ministries staff joins together in prayer. If you have a prayer request for yourself or a loved one, simply write to us.

Administrative Office: 40 Overlook Drive, Chappaqua, New York 10514 Telephone: (914) 769-9000